Challenging Racism

Editor: Danielle Lobban

Volume 447

First published by Independence Educational Publishers

The Studio, High Green

Great Shelford

Cambridge CB22 5EG

England

© Independence 2024

Copyright

This book is sold subject to the condition that it shall not, by way of trade or otherwise, be lent, resold, hired out or otherwise circulated in any form of binding or cover other than that in which it is published without the publisher's prior consent.

Photocopy licence

The material in this book is protected by copyright. However, the purchaser is free to make multiple copies of particular articles for instructional purposes for immediate use within the purchasing institution. Making copies of the entire book is not permitted.

ISBN-13: 978 1 86168 907 8

Printed in Great Britain

Pureprint Group

Acknowledgements

The publisher is grateful for permission to reproduce the material in this book. While every care has been taken to trace and acknowledge copyright, the publisher tenders its apology for any accidental infringement or where copyright has proved untraceable. The publisher would be pleased to come to a suitable arrangement in any such case with the rightful owner.

The material reproduced in **issues** books is provided as an educational resource only. The views, opinions and information contained within reprinted material in **issues** books do not necessarily represent those of Independence Educational Publishers and its employees.

Although every effort has been made to ensure that website addresses are correct at time of going to press, Independence Educational Publishers cannot be held responsible for the content of any website mentioned in this book.

Images

Cover image courtesy of iStock. All other images courtesy of Freepik, Pixabay, Pexels, and Unsplash.

Additional acknowledgements

With thanks to the Independence team: Janey Hills, Klaudia Sommer and Jackie Staines.

Danielle Lobban

Cambridge, October 2024

Contents

Chapter 1: What is Racism?

What is racism?	1
What is race?	2
Exploring ethnicity: understanding the difference between ethnicity and race	3
Different types of racism	4
What is the difference between institutional and structural racism?	5
Viewed through history, racism is a lot more black and white	6
The laws on race discrimination in the UK	10
What is 'Global Majority' and why is it replacing 'BAME'?	11

Chapter 2: Racism Today

Whiteness is at the heart of racism in Britain – so why is it portrayed as a Black problem?	12
Racism in Britain is not a black and white issue. It's far more complicated	14
Gypsies are one of the most vulnerable groups in society – why are we still ignored?	16
Black British Voices: the findings	17
Quarter of adults in England have negative view of those flying St George's cross	20
Is the England flag racist?	22
I knew what it was like being black and British – but when I moved to the US, I was called the N-word for the first time	23
The 'anti-racists' want me to hate Britain	24
The delusion of racial tolerance in the UK	25
Over a third of people from minority groups have experienced racist assaults, survey finds	27
Enough is enough: calling an end to racist points-scoring	28
'Pervasive and relentless' racism on the rise in Europe, survey finds	29

Chapter 3: Fighting Racism

Turning awareness into action: how you can challenge racism	31
Blackout Tuesday: the black square is a symbol of online activism for non-activists	32
Performative allyship is deadly – here's what to do instead	34
Windrush scandal explained	36
The Windrush generation hero who fought racism and won	38
How to be anti-racist	40
Ways to fight against racism	41

Further Reading/Useful Websites	42
Glossary	43
Index	44

Introduction

Challenging Racism is volume 447 in the **issues** series. The aim of the series is to offer current, diverse information about important issues in our world, from a UK perspective.

About *Challenging Racism*

Over a third of people from minority groups have experienced racist assaults in the UK. This book explores different types of racism, who experiences racism, why it happens, and how it can be prevented.

Our sources

Titles in the **issues** series are designed to function as educational resource books, providing a balanced overview of a specific subject.

The information in our books is comprised of facts, articles and opinions from many different sources, including:

- Newspaper reports and opinion pieces
- Website factsheets
- Magazine and journal articles
- Statistics and surveys
- Government reports
- Literature from special interest groups.

A note on critical evaluation

Because the information reprinted here is from a number of different sources, readers should bear in mind the origin of the text and whether the source is likely to have a particular bias when presenting information (or when conducting their research). It is hoped that, as you read about the many aspects of the issues explored in this book, you will critically evaluate the information presented.

It is important that you decide whether you are being presented with facts or opinions. Does the writer give a biased or unbiased report? If an opinion is being expressed, do you agree with the writer? Is there potential bias to the 'facts' or statistics behind an article?

Activities

Throughout this book, you will find a selection of assignments and activities designed to help you engage with the articles you have been reading and to explore your own opinions. Some tasks will take longer than others and there is a mixture of design, writing and research-based activities that you can complete alone or in a group.

Further research

At the end of each article we have listed its source and a website that you can visit if you would like to conduct your own research. Please remember to critically evaluate any sources that you consult and consider whether the information you are viewing is accurate and unbiased.

Issues Online

The **issues** series of books is complemented by our online resource, issuesonline.co.uk

On the Issues Online website you will find a wealth of information, covering over 75 topics, to support the PSHE and RSE curriculum.

Why Issues Online?

Researching a topic? Issues Online is the best place to start for...

Librarians

Issues Online is an essential tool for librarians: feel confident you are signposting safe, reliable, user-friendly online resources to students and teaching staff alike. We provide multi-user concurrent access, so no waiting around for another student to finish with a resource. Issues Online also provides FREE downloadable posters for your shelf/wall/table displays.

Teachers

Issues Online is an ideal resource for lesson planning, inspiring lively debate in class, and setting lessons and homework tasks.

Our accessible, engaging content helps deepen students' knowledge, promotes critical thinking, and develops independent learning skills.

Issues Online saves precious preparation time. We wade through the wealth of material on the internet to filter the best quality, most relevant and up-to-date information you need to start exploring a topic.

Our carefully selected, balanced content presents an overview and insight into each topic from a variety of sources and viewpoints.

Students

Issues Online is designed to support your studies in a broad range of topics, particularly social issues relevant to young people today.

There are thousands of articles, statistics and infographs instantly available to help you with homework, research, and assignments.

With 24/7 access using the powerful Algolia search system, you can find relevant information quickly, easily and safely anytime from your laptop, tablet or smartphone, in class or at home.

Visit issuesonline.co.uk to find out more!

Chapter 1

What is Racism?

What is racism?

In today's world, one of the biggest challenges we face is understanding and addressing the issue of racism. Racism is a complex topic that can sometimes feel overwhelming, but it is important for everyone – especially young people – to grasp what it means and how it affects society. Learning about racism is not just about recognising how it harms individuals and communities, but also about how each of us can contribute to a fairer, more inclusive world.

Understanding racism: the basics

At its simplest, racism is when someone is treated unfairly or discriminated against because of their race or ethnicity. It is based on the belief that some races are better than others, and this idea leads to negative attitudes, prejudice, and harmful behaviours. Racism can show up in many forms, from offensive comments or stereotypes to more serious actions, like excluding people from opportunities or treating them unfairly just because of their race.

There are two main types of racism: individual and systemic. Individual racism refers to the attitudes, beliefs, and actions of a person towards someone of a different race. For example, making fun of someone's accent or assuming negative things about someone based on their skin colour are examples of individual racism. Systemic racism, on the other hand, is when racism is built into the rules, policies, or practices of institutions, such as schools, workplaces, or the Government. This type of racism can be harder to see, but it has long-lasting effects on groups of people, limiting their access to jobs, education, or even justice.

The impact of racism

Racism doesn't just hurt the people who are directly targeted; it harms society as a whole. For individuals, racism can lead to feelings of anger, fear, and hopelessness. It can also affect their mental and physical health, causing stress, anxiety, and even depression. People who experience racism might also face obstacles in education or employment, which can limit their opportunities and reduce their quality of life.

For society, racism creates divisions between people and fuels misunderstanding and mistrust. When certain groups are held back by discrimination, it wastes talent and potential. Think of all the people who might not get the chance to achieve their goals just because of their race or background. In addition, racism can lead to social unrest and conflict, as people fight against unfair treatment and demand equality.

Why racism exists

Racism often comes from ignorance, fear, or a lack of understanding. Many people hold racist beliefs because they have been taught to think this way, or because they have grown up in environments where racist ideas are common. Stereotypes – oversimplified ideas about groups of people – also play a big role in spreading racism. These stereotypes can be seen in the media, in jokes, or in everyday conversations, and they shape how people view each other.

How we can fight racism

The good news is that racism can be challenged and changed. Education is one of the most powerful tools we have to combat racism. By learning about different cultures, histories, and experiences, we can break down stereotypes and replace ignorance with understanding. Speaking out when you see racism happening, even in small ways, is another important step. Every time we challenge racism, we make it harder for these ideas to thrive.

Change starts with all of us. By educating ourselves and others, by being open to conversations about race, and by actively supporting equality, we can build a society where everyone is respected and valued, no matter their race or background.

What is race?

What is race?

In our intricate and diverse world, understanding the concept of *race* is both an intellectual and social necessity. It's a topic plastered across headlines and dissected in schools, yet it remains widely misunderstood or oversimplified. This exploration aims to shed light on what race is, its history, and its importance, using language and examples suitable for teenage readers.

The basics of race

At first glance, race appears to be a straightforward category based on physical characteristics such as skin colour, hair texture, and facial features. It might seem natural to classify people into different races based on these visible traits. However, underneath this superficial assessment lies a complex and contested concept that spans disciplines, including biology, sociology, and history.

Race is not just skin-deep. It is a social construct. This means that rather than being an unchangeable or scientific trait, race has been created and defined by societies and cultures. Over centuries, people have been grouped and regrouped into different races based on changing criteria, which are influenced by political, social, and economic factors.

A brief history of racial thinking

The idea of categorising people based on their physical appearance isn't new. However, the concept of race as we understand it today began to take shape during the age of exploration and colonialism, from the 15th century onwards. European explorers and colonisers encountered people with different cultures, languages, religions, and appearances than their own. To justify the conquering of lands and the oppression of these people, Europeans developed the notion of race, ranking people in a hierarchy with themselves at the top.

Scientific racism in the 19th and early 20th centuries further cemented racial categories. Scientists inaccurately claimed that races had different intellectual, moral, and physical capabilities. These debunked theories fuelled imperial conquests, slavery, and discrimination.

Race is a social construct

Despite the historical use of race to categorise and divide, modern science has dismantled the notion that significant genetic differences exist amongst races. The Human Genome Project, an endeavour that mapped the entire human DNA sequence, revealed that all humans share 99.9% of their genetic makeup, regardless of their race. This underscores that the concept of race is not about biological differences but about how societies perceive and react to differences.

So, if race is a social construct, why does it matter? It matters because societies have built systems and structures around this concept, which have real and lasting effects on people's lives. Race influences opportunities, resources, treatment by the legal and healthcare systems, and personal interactions. It shapes identities, experiences, and the way people see the world and are seen by it.

Understanding racism

Since race plays such a significant role in societies, it's impossible to talk about it without discussing racism. Racism is the belief in the superiority of one race over another, which often results in discrimination and prejudice towards people based on their race or ethnicity. While anyone can harbour prejudice, racism, particularly in the form of institutional racism, involves the power to affect individuals' lives through laws, societal norms, and practices.

The importance of celebrating diversity

Acknowledging and celebrating racial and cultural diversity is crucial in combating racism. It involves recognising and valuing the unique experiences, perspectives, and contributions of people from different backgrounds. Celebrating diversity not only helps in understanding and respecting others but also enriches societies by fostering creativity, empathy, and inclusivity.

The impact of race on identity

For many, race is an important aspect of their identity, influencing how they see themselves and how others perceive them. It can be a source of pride, community, and strength but also a target for discrimination and prejudice. Balancing the personal significance of race with the awareness that it is a social construct can be complex. However, it is a crucial part of navigating social interactions and understanding one's place in the world.

Moving forward

Understanding race requires us to navigate a landscape strewn with historical injustices, ongoing inequalities, and complex social dynamics. It calls for introspection, honesty, and a willingness to learn and unlearn. By engaging with these discussions, we can hope to dismantle prejudices and build more inclusive societies.

In conclusion, race is far more than the physical differences apparent at a glance. It is a profound, complex issue rooted in history, shaped by power dynamics and societal beliefs, and with ongoing implications for individuals and communities worldwide. Understanding race – and the systems of privilege and oppression connected to it – is critical as we strive towards a world that celebrates diversity and promotes equality. Remember, the journey towards this understanding is continuous, and every step taken to educate oneself and challenge personal prejudices counts.

In recognising the construct of race and the pervasive impact of racism, we're equipped to foster a more inclusive, empathetic, and equitable society. For teenagers stepping into a world bustling with diverse perspectives and identities, approaching race with an open mind and heart is not just beneficial – it's essential.

Exploring ethnicity: understanding the difference between ethnicity and race

Understanding the difference: race vs. ethnicity

When you're chatting with friends, scrolling through social media, or even filling out forms for school or sports, you might come across the terms 'race' and 'ethnicity.' Although a lot of people use them interchangeably, they're not the same thing. Each term has its own unique meaning and significance. To make sense of it all, let's break down what race and ethnicity mean and how they affect our understanding of identity and culture.

What is race?

Imagine you're looking at a rainbow. You see different colours, right? In a basic sense, race is like those colours – it's a way humans have classified each other based on physical characteristics, like skin colour, eye shape, and hair texture. Societies created categories of race, predominantly to distinguish people by their outward features. But, unlike the distinct colours of a rainbow that you can clearly see, race is not scientifically defined by biology. Instead, it's a social concept that's changed over time and varies across different parts of the world.

Throughout history, people used the idea of race to include or exclude groups of people and, unfortunately, to justify unequal treatment – a system known as racism. It's like labelling all apples as either red or green when in reality, there are loads of different shades and types of apples out there.

What is ethnicity?

While race focuses on the physical, ethnicity is all about culture. It encompasses the traditions, language, nationality, religion, and heritage that a group of people share. Think of ethnicity as the music of a specific group; it's the shared melody and rhythm of language, food, family traditions, and even the holidays they celebrate.

For example, someone might be racially categorised as 'Asian,' but their ethnicity could be Chinese, Korean, or Vietnamese. Each of these ethnic groups has its own cultural practices, languages, and experiences that make them unique.

Why it matters

Understanding the distinction between race and ethnicity is important because it helps us appreciate the rich tapestry of human diversity. When we box people into racial categories without regard to ethnicity, we miss out on the beautiful details of their cultural backgrounds and personal stories.

Imagine going to an art gallery where all the paintings are labelled simply by the dominant colour. You'd miss out on the styles, textures, and intentions of the artists – the very essence of their work. Similarly, when we learn to appreciate both racial and ethnic differences, we see people in their full complexity and beauty.

So, how do they intersect?

Race and ethnicity are like two threads woven together in the fabric of identity. A person might identify as black (race) and as Ethiopian (ethnicity). Their experiences, values, and perspectives will be influenced by both their race and their ethnicity. Sometimes race and ethnicity align closely, and other times they may lead to very different experiences and understandings of the world.

Embracing diversity

An essential part of growing up is figuring out your own identity, which includes your race and ethnicity. This also means respecting and learning from others' identities. Everyone has a story shaped by their racial and ethnic background, and these stories deserve to be heard and celebrated.

In a world where you can meet friends from all over the globe with just a click, understanding the nuances of race and ethnicity can help build bridges of understanding and respect. Instead of focusing on what sets us apart, we can celebrate the diversity that enriches our collective human experience.

Final thoughts

Race and ethnicity are complex and can affect how we see each other and ourselves. By digging deeper into these differences, teens can develop greater empathy and appreciation for the unique backgrounds and perspectives of the people around them. Remember, labels should not define us, but understanding them can help us build a world that's more inclusive and full of mutual respect.

So next time you encounter the terms race and ethnicity, think about the broad spectrum of human diversity they represent. And most importantly, remember that every individual is so much more than just a category or a label – they're a person with their own story, just like you.

Different types of racism

Racism, in its simplest form, refers to prejudice, discrimination, or antagonism directed against someone of a different race based on the belief that one's own race is superior. However, the ways in which racism manifests can vary greatly. Let's explore the different types of racism that are prevalent in our world.

1. Individual racism

Individual racism is perhaps the most recognisable form. It occurs when a person harbours prejudicial beliefs about people from different races. Such beliefs might manifest through derogatory language, racial slurs, or through more subtle means such as exclusion or avoiding individuals based on their race. Unfortunately, these attitudes can lead to acts of violence or bullying, severely impacting the lives of victims.

2. Institutional racism

Institutional racism is more systemic and entrenched than individual racism. It occurs within and across organisations and institutions, such as in the legal system, educational establishments, the workplace, and more. This type of racism is reflected in the policies, practices, and procedures that disadvantage certain racial groups while benefitting others. For instance, a study might reveal that students of certain racial backgrounds are disciplined more harshly in schools, or that employment opportunities are disproportionately low for particular races.

3. Structural racism

Structural racism is broader than institutional racism, encompassing the entire system of public policies, institutional practices, cultural representations, and other norms that work in various, often reinforcing ways to perpetuate racial group inequality. It reflects the historical, cultural, social, and economic systems that maintain the superiority of one race over others. For example, the legacy of colonialism and slavery has created long-term effects on black and ethnic minority communities, influencing their access to education, employment, and healthcare.

4. Cultural racism

Cultural racism, otherwise known as racial prejudice, is rooted in the belief that certain racial groups' cultural practices, languages, or behaviours are inferior or undesirable. This can manifest in mocking someone's accent, traditions, or even their food. Cultural racism often overlaps with stereotypes, leading to generalisations about individuals based on their racial or ethnic backgrounds. These stereotypes can be damaging and limit a person's ability to express their personal identity freely.

5. Colourism

Colourism is a form of prejudice or discrimination in which people are treated differently based on the social meanings attached to skin colour. Colourism can occur within a racial group, where lighter skin is often favoured over darker skin. This prejudice can affect one's opportunities in life, including employment, relationships, and within the justice system, reinforcing a narrow standard of beauty and acceptability.

6. Environmental racism

Environmental racism refers to the way in which minority group neighbourhoods (populated primarily by people of colour and the economically disadvantaged) are burdened with a disproportionate number of hazards, including toxic waste facilities, garbage dumps, and other sources of environmental pollution and foul odours. It showcases how racism can be deeply embedded in societal structures, affecting even the quality of air and water that people have access to.

Tackling racism

Understanding the different facets of racism is the first step towards tackling it. Each form of racism requires specific strategies for change, from altering individual behaviours and attitudes to overhauling systemic and institutional policies. Education plays a crucial role in combatting racism. Learning about diverse cultures, histories, and perspectives can foster understanding and respect among individuals from different racial backgrounds.

Empathy is also vital. Trying to understand and relate to the experiences of those who have been affected by racism can drive positive change in how we interact with one another. It's about recognising that despite our differences in appearance, culture, or heritage, we share common humanity.

Lastly, speaking out against racism when we witness it can make a significant difference. Whether it's a racist joke, a discriminatory policy, or an act of violence, challenging racism in all its forms is essential to creating a more equitable and just society.

What is the difference between institutional and structural racism?

The Commission on Race and Ethnic Disparities' report, which found 'no evidence of institutional racism', has been widely criticised.

By Ellie Abraham

A report by the independent Commission on Race and Ethnic Disparities, released on 31 March 2021, concluded that although racism and instances of racial injustice still exist in the UK, 'we no longer see a Britain where the system is deliberately rigged against ethnic minorities.'

The controversial report has sparked nationwide conversations, especially against the claim that there is 'no evidence of institutional racism' and that, although the UK is not a 'post-racial society', it sets a good example for other white-majority countries when it comes to diversity.

Speaking on BBC Radio 4's *Today* show on Wednesday, the commission's chairman Dr Tony Sewell claimed there was no evidence of institutional racism in the UK and that the phrase is wrongly used.

He said: 'What we have seen is that the term institutional racism is sometimes wrongly applied and it's been a sort of catch-all phrase for microaggressions or acts of racial abuse.'

To understand what institutional racism is, we must first understand what structural racism is – the two terms are interconnected but differ slightly.

What is structural racism?

Structural racism encompasses all of the social, political and economic systems of our society collectively. It is how large-scale systems, historic and contemporary ideologies, social forces and processes combine and manifest in inequality between racial groups.

Kehinde Andrews, the UK's professor of Black Studies at Birmingham City University told *The Independent*: 'Structural racism refers to the systematic oppression of ethnic minorities that leads the disparities that we see in terms of income, employment, health, etc.

'So the disproportionate death rates from Covid-19 are an example of structural racism, caused by the place we [ethnic minorities] find ourselves in society – more likely to live in inner-city, key workers, working-class.'

In the workplace, executive positions held disproportionately by white individuals are an outcome of structural racism, which is upheld by institutional racism in education, the workplace, as well as other areas of society. Ethnic minorities are more likely to be in low-paid, insecure jobs.

According to Andrews, 'the wealth gap is probably the area of the clearest structural racism as it locks in so much of the disparities.'

What is institutional racism?

Institutional racism is racism that exists in institutional settings and is typically political or social. Through policies and practices, whether done consciously or unconsciously, the outcomes disadvantage one racial group.

Andrews explained: 'Institutional racism refers to how racism is practised through the institutions such as schools, universities, workplaces in ways that maintain structural racism.'

In 1999, the Metropolitan Police was investigated over its handling of the murder of black teenager Stephen Lawrence. It was found by Sir William Macpherson, who led the public inquiry, to be institutionally racist.

Macpherson described it as 'the collective failure of an organisation to provide an appropriate and professional service to people because of their colour, culture or ethnic origin.'

He added that institutional racism can be seen in 'processes, attitudes and behaviour which amount to discrimination through unwitting prejudice, ignorance, thoughtlessness and racist stereotyping which disadvantages minority ethnic people'.

Examples of this can be seen in policing – in October 2020, figures showed black people were more than nine times more likely to be stopped and searched by the police than white people.

Additionally, Andrews said: 'Institutional racism in the education system means that black people are more likely to leave university qualified, and the institutional racism in the workplace means that qualified black graduates are less likely to be employed.

'The worst way to look at institutional racism is to focus on just one sector, as all of these problems are interlinked.'

1 April 2021

The above information is reprinted with kind permission from *The Independent*.

© independent.co.uk 2024

www.independent.co.uk

Viewed through history, racism is a lot more black and white

'Ignore populists and simplistic definitions, history should be central to our understanding of racism.' – PhD historian Joe Hopkinson explores today's misconceptions of 'racism' and considers its history in the wake of the murder of George Floyd in the United States and the outcry that has since followed.

Watching the protests and riots in the US in the wake of the murder of George Floyd made me write down a few thoughts that turned into this essay about race and racism in Britain. I am a PhD candidate in History at the University of Huddersfield studying the history of multicultural education in Britain through the perspectives of those who experienced it as children. As I have been privileged enough to receive such an expensive education, I've been able to develop a perspective on race over the last few years that may help some to think about and understand the current situation. In this essay, I attempt to link academic theories about race with contemporary circumstances, discuss why people misunderstand racism, and to explain how race is a historical force which we must all attempt to understand if we are to engage properly with current events.

Like many others watching in the UK, I am disgusted by the situation in the US following the recent murder of George Floyd, but as a British person it is easy to feel righteously angry about racism in the US while putting almost no thought into racism at home. Black or Asian British reporters are for instance reprimanded for speaking the truth about Donald Trump and false accusations of racism are thrown back at Black or Asian British MPs who're simply describing the racism they and their communities have experienced at the hands of white people throughout history. I think that a big part of the problem is that few people understand racism for what it is. They might know the simplistic definition of the word but are unable to perceive it through the lens of history. If you don't understand the history of race and racism then you won't understand that white supremacy was the mainstream way of thinking until recently, and you might be unable to fully fathom why people are so angry about many of the things that are happening today.

'But why make it about colour? Everyone can be racist!'

The dictionary or Wikipedia definition of racism strips the word of its true historical meaning: 'prejudice, discrimination, or antagonism directed against someone of a different race based on the belief that one's own race is superior'. A child reading that might think it is talking about a phenomenon that each human population group has participated in equally throughout history, an entirely understandable but false assumption. At this moment, it might be worth pointing out that race is a social construct with far less scientific basis than most people actually think. Similarly, ethnicity is another concept that is used to define human difference that is more of a social construct than a scientific way to divide peoples; however, it relates to cultural identities that people choose whereas race is a category that was invented and imposed by white people. From the fifteenth to sixteenth centuries onwards, white Europeans began categorising human populations through racial hierarchies which placed white people at the top, and darker skinned people at the bottom. As you hopefully know already, this led to serious worldwide consequences including the most devastating genocide and wars to have taken place to date. After 1945, the world slowly started talking less and less about race and more in terms of ethnicity. Scientists from the United Nations Educational, Scientific and Cultural Organization made a series of declarations from 1950 onwards about how we should not use the concept of race anymore because it had led to people thinking that racial differences were fixed and real. Instead, they advocated talking in terms of ethnicity. As a result, New Racism, also known as cultural racism, emerged. This is racist rhetoric that avoids overtly racial terms using ambiguous phrasing and an emphasis upon cultural difference as opposed to racial. This is a topic that requires its own essay, but it is important to be aware that we have not progressed from old biological racism to racial parity. Racism has not gone away it has just become more complex and covert. Overall, if we're talking about racism – the old style or the new – as a historical force it's not exactly a concept that can be reversed to position white people as the victims unless you're talking hypothetically or about a parallel dimension where Black people enslaved millions of white people over hundreds of years, instead of the other way around.

No one with any sense is saying that white people are the only humans that can be prejudiced. Everyone can be prejudiced. Nevertheless, saying that white people can be the victims of racism misrepresents the word. It may be linguistically correct to say that white people can be the victims of racism if you follow the definition of the term in the dictionary, but it is factually incorrect because in our reality white people are not the victims of the historical force known as racism. Hypothetically, could they be? Yes. But are they? No, that's not what happened. Words matter and I think that the dictionary definition of racism creates a false perception of what it is. Racism has always been something that white Europeans did to the rest of the world. If someone discriminates against you because you're white then you have the right to be upset about it and to seek justice. If you want to describe it as racism that's your business, but hopefully you understand why others feel that you don't really have the right to claim that word.

'People have always been racist, why do whites always get the blame?'

Racism is a specific historical force and type of prejudice that emerged through a belief in racial hierarchies which were developed by white Europeans from the Early Modern era into modernity. Although, proto-forms of racism did emerge in the Middle-Ages. I am not saying that inter-group prejudice was invented by white people towards the end of the 1400s – humans have always grouped together, discriminated against or warred with other groups and the phenomenon we now describe as genocide is as old as history itself – but in the 1400s white Europeans did invent the printing press and navigate the Atlantic to land in the Americas. The combination of the two is significant because at the moment in history when Europeans first began to interact with indigenous peoples on a global scale, they also invented the means to widely spread images and stereotypes about them. The ideology of race and the effects of racism rapidly began to spread at that moment in history.

Human groups have of course understood and noted differences between each other in the past but their ideas on this were quite different to the modern understandings of race. The ancient Greeks for instance understood themselves as Greeks and everyone else as non-Greeks, or Barbarians. During the Middle Ages in Europe, white Europeans interacted regularly with Black African, middle eastern, and Asian groups. They were certainly aware of what became known as racial difference, but they did not articulate it as we do today. Their understanding of human difference was linked to the four humours style of medicine – blood, phlegm, yellow bile, black bile – that remained popular throughout the continent from the Romans until the Renaissance. Those who thought and wrote about human difference during the Medieval period generally believed that the contrasting climates of Africa, Asia, and Europe affected the balance of the four humours therefore creating physical differences that we can see between human groups. Interestingly, pasty white northern Europeans were hypothesised by some back then to be inferior to dark skinned Africans. This was because cold and wet climates were thought to affect the humours by creating slow witted and unathletic people, whereas hot and dry places were believed to do the opposite.

Understandings of race, or raza in Spanish and Portuguese – the first European colonisers and inventors of the modern use of the term – rapidly changed from the late 1400s onwards as Europeans began to conquer, enslave, and otherwise dominate or exploit different populations around the world, all the while writing about the experience and representing it in much of the art that we see in museums across Europe today. Pseudo scientist taxonomists also wrote flawed descriptions of the differences between these groups and developed various racial hierarchies over the centuries in which the whites were invariably at the top and Black Africans at the bottom. These hierarchies and the literary or artistic representations of them created stereotypes that were propagated around Europe and the world by art and the ever-expanding print media. This is why white British people in the 1700s–mid-1900s for instance generally had strong perceptions of Indian and African peoples regardless of whether or not they had actually met anyone from those groups. By the end of the nineteenth century, Europeans dominated the world financially and politically, and the European populace generally believed that their rule over people from far off lands was justified because they were inherently superior in a biological sense.

'But isn't racism a thing of the past?'

To understand current events, you have to know that until very recently the vast majority of Western populations thoroughly and overtly believed in racial hierarchies and white supremacy. Most presumed and acted on the belief that whites were superior to other groups. Today, this is not the case. Your average Western politician does not publicly espouse racist views. When and how things changed exactly is an interesting question and to answer it thoroughly would also require a separate essay or book. One theory argues that there was a historical 'break' in the overt acceptance of white supremacy after the Second World War. People saw all the death and realised that it was largely caused by racism. As a result, for the first time in history, the conditions for massive popular antiracist campaigns emerged. There was of course the Civil Rights movement in the US, the end of segregation and the introduction of antiracist laws in the UK from 1965 onwards. Instead of trying to discuss the changes that were taking place in depth, I will use the following points to try and evoke in some way how this was happening in Britain: to my knowledge Britain last had a Prime Minister who overtly held white supremacist views in 1955. While considering pursuing his third re-election Winston Churchill told his cabinet that he wanted to run on the slogan, Keep England White. Churchill was not re-elected, but his suggestion led to no controversy or negative consequences. In contrast, less than two decades later in 1968, Enoch Powell was sacked from his post as Shadow Defence Secretary by Churchill's former party for publicly making a similar argument and using overtly racial terminology. The circumstances were different but it is clear that something had started to change between those events in 1955 and 1968 in terms of British and global race relations. It would, however, be a massive oversimplification and falsehood to argue that racism in general was somehow disappearing or declining.

We tend to think that racism is less of a problem today because those who overtly and publicly uphold white supremacist views have become an extremist minority. That's a comforting thought for some. It suggests progress. But when you realise that overt, biological, old-style racism was the widely accepted norm until very recently, it seems overly optimistic to assume that we no longer have a problem with racism in the UK or elsewhere. Of the millions of British people who agreed with Enoch Powell in 1968 – reported at the time as a majority of the population – how many are alive today, and how many raised their children to uphold similar views? Overt old-school racism is in my opinion continuing its slow descent into obscurity, in Britain at least, but does that even matter when the economic consequences of racism remain so apparent? Of course things are not the same in the UK as the US, we have different histories, but you only need to have a quick look at the 2017 Race Disparity Audit report to see that racial inequality persists in the UK to a shocking degree. I have spoken with BAME British people who lived through the Sixties and Seventies that see the overt style of racism as dying out, but also that covert racism persists and is more damaging in reality. One African Caribbean man told me that he even preferred it back in the 1970s when he knew who his enemies were because they called him racial slurs to his face. Covert racism is alive and well in the UK today and another topic that deserves its own essay or book. It denies people equal access to housing, jobs, education and causes greater damage to a person's life than experiencing racial abuse in the street or at school. Darker skinned people do not go to British prisons in higher numbers, or achieve less than other groups at British schools because they think it is a good idea and choose to do so. Experts have highlighted for years how these issues are caused by systemic racism but time and time again little of significance changes. As Professor David Gillborn argues, when experts repeatedly highlight that racism is the most salient problem for certain BAME children in British schools, yet the government and educators make few substantial changes, it essentially amounts to a conspiracy against Black people in this country.

I wrote this because I think that more people need to understand and accept the severity of racism in the recent past, so that they can properly understand what is happening in the world today. If you go about thinking of racism in the terms it is defined by in the dictionary, as opposed to understanding it as something historical, you're going to misinterpret what is going on and not get why people are so angry. Similarly, if you're getting triggered by things like #BlackLivesMatter and feel the need to say All

Lives Matter then you're missing the point and falling for Right-wing media narratives that make minoritised people seem like the bad guys when they're just standing up for themselves. On a separate note, I'm regularly infuriated to see so many people indulging themselves on social media in 'researching' ridiculous conspiracy theories online. There are so many people out there who seem to position themselves as against the establishment who will argue until they're blue in the face that 'they' are controlling us in different ways. Yet, for one reason or another, they don't seem to think that racism is even worth discussing when it's one of the biggest and most real conspiracies out there – I guess it doesn't help that many of their conspiracies have roots in Antisemitism.

'Well I support their cause but don't approve of riots!'

I wish nothing but good luck to all of the protesters in the US right now and hope that people in Britain are watching what is happening and taking a long hard think about strengthening efforts to improve the situation at home. I also wish that white British people could react as optimistically and with the same level of dignity to accusations of racism, or the suggestion that they take part in a racist system, as BAME British have often done when suffering actual instances of racial prejudice. The amount of visible minoritised British people I have interviewed who take an incredibly sanguine view of the horrific racism they experienced as children and throughout their lives is surprising. I'm regularly told by the first and second generation African Caribbean, South Asian, or Chinese British people I speak with that they always felt they had a duty to integrate and become British, but the rest of their stories often suggest that this was not reciprocated by white British society. I am certainly not saying that reacting passively to racism is a good thing, but through speaking to those who experience racism I can see that the day-to-day reality of resisting it must be incredibly emotionally complex and draining. The violence we are now seeing in the US is far from the normal reaction. It may seem like an extreme reaction to one event, but in reality it is a very understandable reaction to countless abuses. My point is that we all need to work together to end racism but visible minoritised people and communities have been doing more than their fair share of the work. Every time you see a race related riot remember that the people taking part have probably experienced numerous racial slights throughout their lives. Every time they turned the other cheek, refused to rock the boat, and ignored microaggressions or other racist slights to save their friends/company/colleagues face white people have not exactly reacted by thinking 'hmm, maybe we should treat them better and as equal humans after all'. It should therefore be no surprise when we get serious riots in the UK again.

We had serious nationwide race related riots across Britain in 1981, localised race related riots in 1975, 1985, 1987, 1991, 2001 and most recently the nationwide riots that spread after the shooting of Mark Duggan, a young man of white British and African descent, by police in London in 2011. The ingredients for another serious riot seem to be there today. I know that I would be furious if I was constantly seeing news stories about people demonising my community and religion or deporting my grandparents. All it usually takes to create the spark that lights the fire is one person in a position of authority, usually a police officer, doing something stupid. We're also so tied with the US today that something over there could very well lead to serious consequences over here. Recently, I have seen more and more, predominantly young, British people on social media using the slogan All Cops Are Bastards (usually denoted by the acronym ACAB). I disagree with the sentiment yet understand why people land at that conclusion when they see that the police are protecting a broken system. Remember, while the situation in the US has thematic similarities with the UK it is also substantially different. Our police have their problems, but they are not exactly the same as in the US. Do not get completely caught up in US politics and forget the intricacies of what is happening and has happened over here. They clearly need to completely over-haul their law enforcement somehow. Maybe we will eventually need to do something comparable in the UK, but for me the more pertinent way to solve our problems is for all white British people, not just the police, to reflect deeply on what their ancestors did around the world as a result of racist beliefs that continue to shape our lives today.

Conclusion

We still benefit from the racism, slavery, and colonialism done by white British people over several hundred years and should think with focus about making things right somehow. We need to re-consider teaching antiracism in British schools. A nuanced look at British migration, colonial and decolonisation history should become a mandatory element of the national curriculum as opposed to optional. We do not need to hammer home negative messages or prevent children from taking pride in their British identity, but we do need to create a unifying multicultural British identity that everyone can take pride in moving forward. However, for us to discuss and understand the good things that unify us, we also need to engage with some of the bad that divided us in the past and arguably continues to divide us. You can't for example discuss and commemorate the positive contribution of the Chinese Labour Corps to the British war effort during the First World War without also talking about how a number of the Chinese men who participated were forcibly deported from the UK in the early 1920s, some after already forming families. People balk at the idea of reparations, but we widely accept as a society that we have an inter-generational responsibility to look after our elders by paying taxes that feed their pensions and healthcare, so why don't we also see that we have a similar responsibility to right the wrongs that they and their elders caused, or perpetuated? A good start would be for people to accept the historical relevance of #BlackLivesMatter and to broadly support all efforts to work towards racial parity. For this to happen we need the public to fully comprehend the historic nature of these issues otherwise we will continue to protect an unequal system and repeat past mistakes.

June 2020

The above information is reprinted with kind permission from the University of Huddersfield.
© 2024 University of Huddersfield

www.hud.ac.uk

The laws on race discrimination in the UK

The United Kingdom's journey towards achieving racial equality has been marked by a series of significant legislative milestones. These laws reflect the evolving understanding of what it means to live in a multicultural society where everyone deserves respect, dignity, and equal opportunities, irrespective of their race or ethnicity. Let's take a look at the key legislative milestones that have shaped race relations in the UK.

1965: The Race Relations Act 1965

In 1965, the UK made its first bold step with the introduction of the Race Relations Act. This pioneering legislation aimed to combat racial discrimination in public places, such as hotels and restaurants. It was a symbol of progress, but it was only the first step in a much longer journey.

The Race Relations Board

Following the 1965 Act, the Race Relations Board was established to address grievances related to discrimination. The board was an essential first attempt at creating an institution to protect individuals from racial prejudice, serving as a mediator in disputes over discrimination.

1968: Race Relations Act 1968

Building on its predecessor, the Race Relations Act of 1968 expanded protections against discrimination to cover employment and housing. It showed further commitment against racism but also highlighted the need for more robust enforcement mechanisms.

1976: Race Relations Act 1976

A significant stride was taken in 1976 with the Race Relations Act, encompassing a broader scope than ever before. This time, the Act tackled not only direct discrimination but also indirect forms that might occur unintentionally, but still have the effect of disadvantaging people because of their race. It was a transformative piece of legislation that echoed a deepening understanding of racial dynamics.

Commission for Racial Equality

The 1976 Act also led to the formation of the Commission for Racial Equality (CRE), a powerful body tasked with promoting racial equality and challenging racial discrimination across the UK. The CRE played a pivotal role in paving the way towards a more inclusive society.

1984: PACE 1984

While not a race law per se, the Police and Criminal Evidence Act (PACE) 1984 introduced important safeguards against the mistreatment of individuals by the police, which disproportionately affected minority ethnic communities. It reflected growing awareness and concerns over racial biases within the criminal justice system. The PACE Act was created after a public inquiry into the Brixton Riots in 1981.

2000: Race Relations Amendment Act 2000

The new millennium brought with it the Race Relations Amendment Act 2000, significantly amending the 1976 Act. This was largely in response to the inquiry into the murder of Stephen Lawrence, which highlighted institutional racism within the Metropolitan Police. This act placed a legal duty on public bodies to actively promote racial equality, marking a shift from reactive measures to proactive ones.

2006: Equality Act 2006

The Equality Act of 2006 was another pivotal moment, setting up the framework for the creation of the Equality and Human Rights Commission. It started the process of consolidating anti-discrimination laws, including those related to race, into a single piece of legislation.

The Equality and Human Rights Commission

Established under the Equality Act 2006, the Equality and Human Rights Commission (EHRC) took over the responsibilities of the Commission for Racial Equality. The EHRC aims to protect and promote human rights and to uphold equality across the spectrum, including race.

2010: Equality Act 2010

The Equality Act 2010 represents the culmination of decades of efforts, simplifying and strengthening the laws protecting people from discrimination. It consolidated previous anti-discrimination laws, including race laws, into one comprehensive act, making it easier to understand and enforce.

As we look at the progression from the Race Relations Act of 1965 to the Equality Act of 2010, it's clear that the path toward racial equality in the UK has been one of continuous learning, adapting, and striving for a better society. Each piece of legislation has built on the last, reflecting a growing understanding of what is needed to create a truly inclusive community.

These laws are not just historical milestones; they are a testament to the ongoing journey towards equality and understanding. By knowing our past, we can engage in more meaningful conversations about our future, challenging ourselves to build a world where everyone, regardless of race, has the opportunity to thrive.

What is 'Global Majority' and why is it replacing 'BAME'?

One acronym to describe people of Black, Asian, Indigenous or Latin ancestry is falling out of favour - we look at why.

By Nadine White, Race Correspondent

More and more organisations are ditching the term 'BAME' in reference to people of Black, Asian, Indigenous or Latin ancestry, instead opting to use 'Global Majority'.

This week, the National Trust employed the language while announcing a new training initiative geared towards boosting ethnic representation.

But what does 'Global Majority' mean and why has 'BAME' fallen out of favour?

For many, 'BAME' (Black And Minority Ethnic) is clumsy, inaccurate and lumps all people who aren't white under one tiny, sidelined umbrella, while 'Global Majority' is a linguistic attempt to add wider context around their lived experiences; the phrase has been used in the US since the early 2000s, at least.

Moreover, 'BAME' fuels a misconception that people from minoritised communities are inherently marginalised, whereas those with African, Asian, Indigenous or Latin ancestry comprise approximately 85% of the global population.

Nearly 60% of the world's population live on the Asian continent, according to official data, while 18% reside in Africa, 9% in the European continent, 8% across Latin America and the Caribbean, 4% in North America and less than 1% in the Oceania region.

As such, so-called ethnic minorities are pretty much only minorities in Europe.

'Understanding that singular truth may shift the dial, it certainly should permanently disrupt and relocate the conversation on race,' said Rosemary Campbell-Stephens, the academic whose work reportedly led to the 'Global Majority' term being coined. 'I identify as Black, of African Caribbean descent and heritage, specifically, Jamaican parentage. My nationality is British.

'My identity does not exist in relation to whiteness and transcends my geographic place of birth. I am part of the Global Majority.'

Those who argue in favour of adopting language like 'Global Majority' say it is a way of de-colonising language and pushing back against racism, the notion that people of non-white ethnicities are inferior. Important statistics relating to non-white people, such as population trends or diversity data within institutions, are squashed together which opens floodgates for all manner of misrepresentation and inaccuracies.

'BAME' can allow institutions and society to disguise a lack of representation of some groups, by pointing to the inclusion of others. The false indication of racial equality that this often brings across, a veneer of progress, is where serious problems can take hold. It can enable organisations to apply the jargon sporadically and rest on their laurels while executives boast about how they've met their diversity quota.

Like the National Trust, other organisations have embraced 'Global Majority', including Westminster City Council in 2022 and the National Council of Voluntary Organisations last year. The Church of England's Archbishops' *Anti-Racism Taskforce Report* in 2021 also felt the description 'United Kingdom Minority Ethnic/Global Majority Heritage' (UKME/GMH) was more suitable for us than 'BAME'.

Polling from think-tank British Future the same year found that less than half (47%) of so-called 'BAME' Britons were confident about the meaning of 'BAME' as a term.

Most ethnic minority Britons (54%) agree that more specific hyphenated identities – such as 'Black British' or 'British Asian' – can help to make national identity feel more inclusive of people from different backgrounds, according to the same survey.

Not everyone is a fan of 'Global Majority' though.

Conservative MP John Hayes, who has previously come under fire for criticising anti-racism work, said of the 'Global Majority' label: 'Minorities and majorities are about the context – you can't use the term 'majority' out of context and assume it affords some sort of accurate description.'

'The distortion of language is at the heart of the liberal left agenda. The malevolent minority that control too much of Britain wish to control and limit language as a precursor to limit[ing] what people think. It is deeply sinister and must be resisted at every turn.'

Nevertheless, the Government's own, and controversial, report by the Commission on Race and Ethnic Disparities (CRED) in 2021 denounced the 'BAME' term as 'unhelpful and redundant' – but failed to suggest an alternative.

17 May 2024

The above information is reprinted with kind permission from *The Independent*.
© independent.co.uk 2024

www.independent.co.uk

Racism Today

Chapter 2

Whiteness is at the heart of racism in Britain – so why is it portrayed as a Black problem?

An article from *The Conversation*.

By Meghan Tinsley, Presidential Fellow in Ethnicity and Inequalities, University of Manchester

In 2020, two police officers in Hackney strip-searched a 15-year-old Black girl at her school. Police conducted the search of this child, known as Child Q, without the consent of her parents, without an appropriate adult present (despite this being required by the Police and Criminal Evidence Act 1984), and with the knowledge that she was menstruating.

The subsequent safeguarding review, held in March 2022, concluded that 'racism (whether deliberate or not) was likely to have been an influencing factor in the decision to undertake a strip search.'

The fallout from the case of Child Q has followed a script that is all too familiar. Anti-racist campaigners have pointed to the incident as further evidence that racism remains a problem in contemporary Britain. Teachers at the school in question have expressed shock, reportedly claiming not to have known about the search. The Metropolitan Police has put the two officers directly involved on desk duty.

Each narrative, and each response, focuses squarely on Child Q and on the violence she suffered. There is a reason why this all seems so predictable. Discussions of racism in Britain centre around the experiences and traumas of Black people, but rarely on the perpetrators.

How we talk about racism

When we talk about incidents of racism, the focus – from both individuals and institutions – is often placed on the victim's behaviour or background.

British police have routinely justified using stop and search more often against ethnic minority groups by incorrectly claiming that crime and gang membership among these groups is higher. Research, however, shows that racial bias is at the root of this disproportionate use of stop and search: Black people in Britain are nine times more likely to be affected than white people.

Similarly, discussions around the higher Covid-19 death rates among minority groups puts disproportionate focus on the health problems (vitamin D deficiency, diabetes) in the affected population groups.

Research shows, however, that racism has been a fundamental cause. It explains why minority ethnic people were more likely to be in dangerous, frontline professions; unable to work from home; more likely to face unemployment and deprivation; and more likely to avoid contact with health professionals. Racism is multifaceted.

As writer and academic Gary Younge put it, 'The virus does not discriminate on grounds of race. It didn't need to. Society had done that already.'

How we respond to racism

When incidents of racism make the news, even activists and protesters emphasise, in response to each case, the victim's innocence and vulnerability. In other words, the victim becomes the whole story: Black people themselves are depicted as the source of racism. American sociologist WEB Du Bois identified this impossible situation in 1897 –

over a century ago – when he asked, 'How does it feel to be a problem?'

Left out of the discussion, every time, is whiteness. Black victims of racism are made hypervisible, while white perpetrators are kept invisible. There is power in this invisibility. Because white people are not racialised – they are seen as the default, and any other racial group is seen as 'other' – their experiences are presented as those of individuals: race is not considered a factor in what they do.

When teachers referred Child Q to the police, they denied her the right to be taught and protected from harm. Instead, they treated her as a threat to other students, thereby effectively placing her outside of the educational institution. Research has highlighted how these institutions are characterised by whiteness, in terms of cohort racial makeup and the student experience and outcomes for people of colour.

When the police officers searched Child Q, they denied her the protections that the law guarantees to children. Instead, they treated her as a criminal adult. In the process, they drew, knowingly or not, from a long history of criminalising and dehumanising Black people for the (imagined) protection of white people.

They also engaged, as the safeguarding review noted, in adultification bias, wherein adults consider Black children to be older and less innocent than white children. Police leaders in Tower Hamlets and Hackney have since acknowledged as much.

Whiteness underpins racism. Ignoring whiteness perpetuates its violence. US writer Ijeoma Oluo made this point emphatically after the 2016 US presidential election.

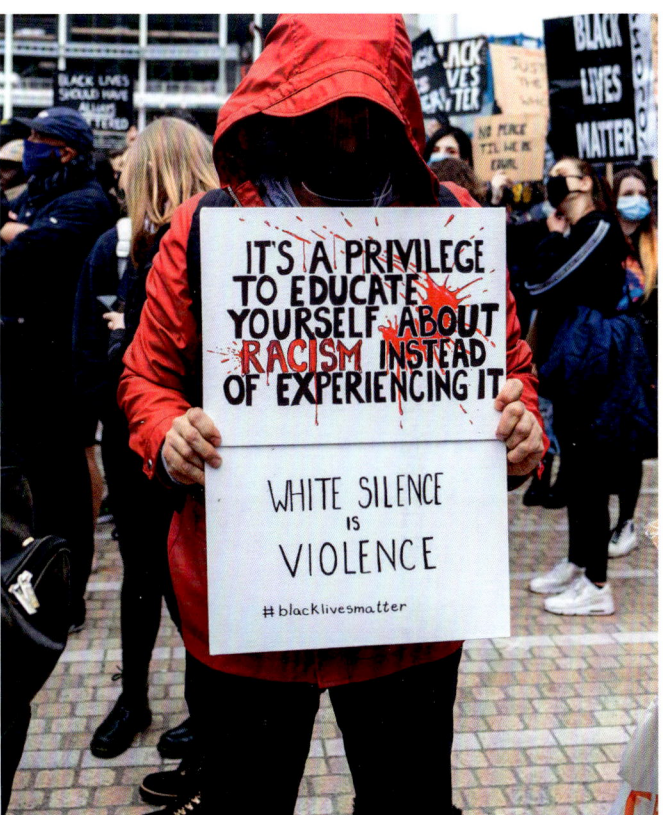

'White people,' she wrote, 'I don't want you to understand me better; I want you to understand yourselves. Your survival has never depended on your knowledge of white culture. In fact, it has required your ignorance.' It is only by making whiteness visible that we can understand what leads to violence against Black people.

At the heart of racism is not the existence of Black people, but the active work of white institutions to maintain white supremacy. White supremacy is bigger than the sum of individual white people's actions.

At its most basic level, whiteness is a way of categorising people, humanising some by dehumanising others. This shapes the way that people exist in society and interact with institutions. It also helps to explain what happened to Child Q. Her statement is a harrowing reminder of how the maintenance of whiteness makes it impossible for Black people to simply exist. 'I can't go a single day,' she said, 'without wanting to scream, shout, cry or just give up.'

Understanding contemporary racism as the legacy of centuries-old colonialism and slavery may make it seem even more overwhelming. But recognising that whiteness is at the heart of racism can and should change our response. Opposing racism means working to overcome whiteness and reclaim humanity.

19 May 2022

THE CONVERSATION

The above information is reprinted with kind permission from *The Conversation*.
© 2010-2024, The Conversation Trust (UK) Limited

www.theconversation.com

Racism in Britain is not a black and white issue. It's far more complicated

A report on ethnic inequality reveals that Irish, Jewish and Traveller people are among the most abused.

By Tomiwa Owolade

Something was amiss but I couldn't say why. I was a sixth-form student and talking to a girl who told me with utter confidence that 'white people can't be victims of racism'. Racism is about power and privilege. White people have power and privilege. Black people and Asians don't. This means that only the latter group can be victims of racism; racism is the exercise of power and privilege against people of colour.

I nodded at the time – she almost convinced me. Almost. I admired her clarity but felt her account was too neat. I liked her passion but thought it was painfully misguided.

It has only been over the past few years that I have been able to say exactly why she is wrong; why her account of racism is provincial rather than progressive; why combating material inequalities should be based on truth rather than distorted narratives.

The year 2021 was a strange time to be alive. The interregnum between lockdown and 'back to normal'. The last full year of Boris Johnson's slipshod government. The terrifying wildfires in Australia. Amid the chaos and change, though, something else seismic occurred that year. More than 14,000 people took part in the Evidence for Equality National Survey between February and October. They came from 21 ethnic backgrounds and all parts of the country. The survey report was released last week, and it claims to be the most comprehensive account of racial inequality in Britain for more than 25 years.

The research was carried out by academics from the universities of St Andrews, Manchester and King's College London, and published in a book called *Racism and Ethnic Inequality in a Time of Crisis*.

Nissa Finney is a professor of human geography at St Andrews and led the report. She argues that the 'UK is immeasurably far from being a racially just society. The kinds of inequality we see in our study would not be there if we had a really just society.'

The figure from the report that has most grabbed the headlines is this: more than a third of ethnic minority people in Britain have experienced some form of racist abuse.

The two groups most likely to say they have experienced racist abuse are Traveller communities and Jewish people.

The standard progressive response would be that this is awful but not surprising. We all know we live in a racist society; anyone who denies this is deluded and complicit with racism. Any racial abuse against any individual is morally abhorrent, and civil society has a moral duty to oppose prejudice. We should try to get the number of people who experience racism as close to zero as we possibly can. But something again nagged at me in the way many have presented the evidence from this survey. Because the corollary of one third of ethnic minority people reporting that they have experienced racist assault is that two thirds of ethnic minority people have not.

This does not mean that there is no racism in Britain. The recent Casey report, for instance, affirmed the existence of institutional racism in the Metropolitan Police. But the Evidence for Equality National Survey report complicates some of the underlying assumptions that many ostensibly progressive people espouse on racial inequality in Britain. One is a narrow idea of what constitutes racism.

Anyone who is white is privileged, we are told, and racism only affects people of colour. The problem with this view is that there are certain minorities who are seen as white and yet experience prejudice. In fact, the two groups most likely to say they have experienced racist abuse, according to the

More than a third of people from ethnic and religious minorities have experienced some form of racist assault

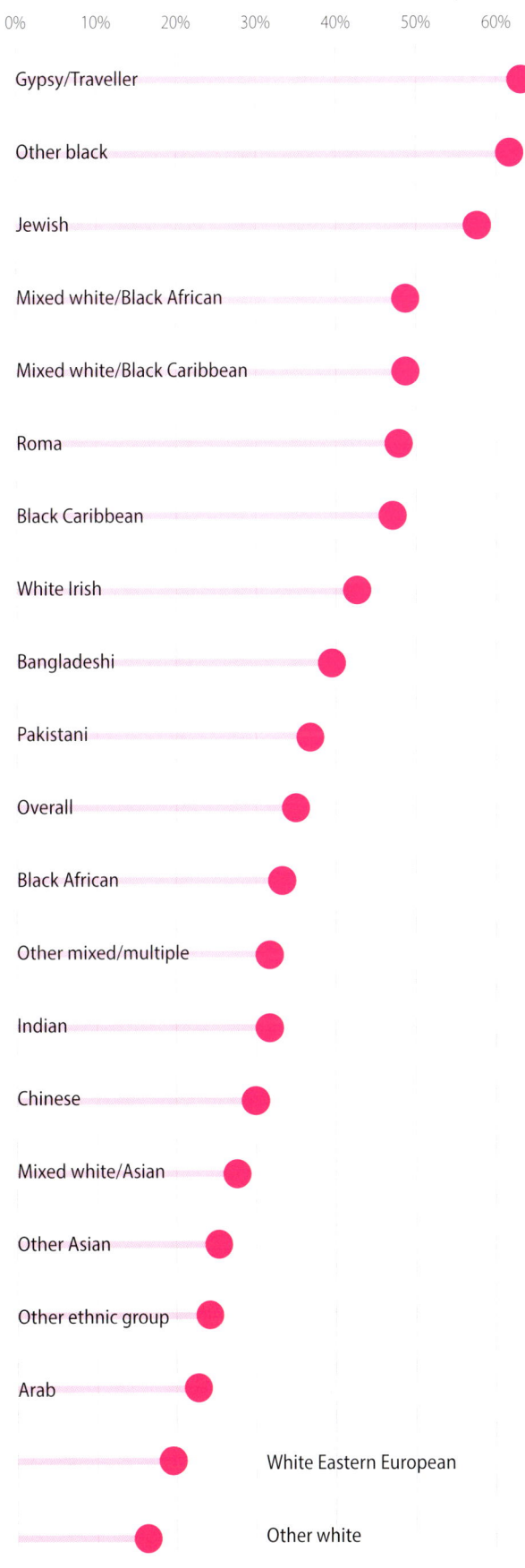

% experiencing racist insults, property damage or physical attacks prior to the pandemic

Source: Evidence for Equality National Survey

survey, are Gypsy, Traveller and Roma communities and Jewish people.

More than 60% of Gypsy and Traveller people reported that they had experienced some form of racist assault. More than 55% of Jewish people report the same.

But we also find striking differences within groups we often unthinkingly group together.

White Irish people are more likely to say they have experienced prejudice in Britain than Black African people.

Black Caribbean people, for instance, are more likely than Black African people to say they have experienced racism – nearly 50% for Black Caribbean people and more than 30% for Black African people. Which also means that more than half of Black Caribbean people and two thirds of Black African people say they experienced no racist assault. All of this from a survey many have used to conclude that Britain is far from being a racially just society.

Remarkably, the survey found that 40% of white Irish people reported experiencing some form of racist assault in their lives. This means that white Irish people are more likely to say they have experienced prejudice in Britain than Black African people and all Asian ethnic groups: Indian, Pakistani, Bangladeshi, Chinese and other Asian groups.

One response to this is obvious. Some minority groups might under-report their experience of racist abuse, others might over-report. We shouldn't take the survey as an objective account of racism in Britain. But the problem with this point of view is that the report has already been used to advance the claim that Britain is still plagued by racism – and the very same people who make this claim also emphasise only one kind of racial inequality, one that puts black and Asian people at the very bottom of society, and 'white' people at the top.

If the latter is true, then we need to discard the report as useless. If the report is useful, we need to recalibrate how we think about racism. We can't think both that the report is helpful and still cling to that narrow account of racism.

There are racial inequalities in our society. This much is true. But this should be approached with subtlety rather than simplicity. This is because ethnic minority people in this country have diverse experiences and any commitment to fighting racial disadvantage needs to incorporate this complex truth if it wants to be truly effective.

Morally speaking, racism is a black and white issue. But when it comes to how it manifests itself, it is multidimensional. The most comprehensive survey on racial inequality for nearly 30 years needs to be examined comprehensively.

15 April 2023

The above information is reprinted with kind permission from *The Guardian*.
© 2024 Guardian News and Media Limited

www.theguardian.com

Gypsies are one of the most vulnerable groups in society – why are we still ignored?

It's almost as if we've hit a point where we know there are racial inequalities, but we're going to pick and choose which ones we want to challenge.

By Katie Alexander

As a member of the Traveller community, I've been told my whole life to shield who I am from the outside world. My parents, my mum especially, would always tell my siblings and I how people would see and treat us differently once they knew of our heritage. Growing up on a council estate in southeast London in the early 2000s, I didn't see myself as any different to anyone else.

When I was around nine years old, I lost my first 'friend' because of my heritage. I didn't understand. I lived in a house with my married parents, just like she did. How could I be so different? And not only different, but bad. How could who I am be so bad that she could not speak to me again?

It is not right for any child to have to comprehend that they are not worthy of another child's friendship because of their race. We do not choose the family or heritage we are born into, yet we have to suffer with the lifelong consequences of inequality. After that point, I began to shut out everyone else around me. While I could not deny who I was, I could hide it to the best of my abilities. It wasn't until I was about 19 that I started being more vocal about my identity.

I am fortunate and privileged that I do not, usually, receive any racist comments to my face. For the most part, I look white and I know this protects me from a lot. However, it doesn't protect me from indirect racism – which, unfortunately, happens a lot. I've been in countless situations where my friends, colleagues and even romantic partners have made racist comments about Travellers. They do not realise the person standing next to them is a part of the group they're insulting.

Recently, someone referred to me as a 'fringe member' of the Traveller community. By this, I'm assuming they mean that I live in a house and don't have a big, fat wedding to go to every week. Oh, and I don't wander down country lanes with a tambourine, so I guess I am a 'fringe member'.

My point is that if these insults were made to another disadvantaged group, they would be shut down, and rightly so. I couldn't imagine anyone referring to someone who is mixed race as a fringe person of colour. Or that someone who is bisexual is not quite gay enough to be a full, legitimate member of the LGBT+ community. It's absolute nonsense.

While movements like Black Lives Matter continue to thrive, the Gypsy community faces increasingly aggressive stigma from wider society. Only a few months ago, we heard comedian Jimmy Carr referring to the 'positive' of the Holocaust being the brutal slaughter of 500,000 Roma and Sinti people.

While there was instant outrage from the community and external allies, there have been no consequences for Jimmy's words. The whole situation seemed to blow over after a weekend, and it was done with. Again, I cannot state the importance of how different society's reaction to this would have been had it been about another minority group.

It's almost as if we've hit a point where we know there are racial inequalities, but we're going to pick and choose which ones we want to challenge. There's also the ongoing issue that many people do not consider Gypsies as a race or group of people, so therefore you can't discriminate against them.

In turn, we leave the most vulnerable groups even more marginalised and silenced than they already were. While living in a world that actively shuns racism, society does not see Gypsies. It does not hear Gypsies. And when people do, they don't care enough to take any form of progressive action.

2 May 2022

> It is not right for any child to have to comprehend that they are not worthy of another child's friendship because of their race.

The above information is reprinted with kind permission from *The Independent*.
© independent.co.uk 2024

www.independent.co.uk

Black British Voices: the findings

The largest survey to date of the opinions and attitudes of Black people in Britain has revealed a central split on the question of British pride.

Around half (49%) of Black Britons consider themselves at least somewhat 'proud to be British', while almost half (45%) take little to no pride in Britishness.

The research also suggests that racial prejudice and insensitivity in UK workplaces remains entrenched, with a high percentage of respondents (88%) saying they have experienced racial discrimination at work.

In fact, almost all (98%) of those surveyed said they have compromised self-expression and identity to fit into the workplace – by adapting speech or hairstyles, for example – with appearance and cultural background cited as factors influencing lack of promotion or development.

The research has been conducted by the University of Cambridge's Department of Sociology in collaboration with The Voice, Britain's only national newspaper for Black communities, and London-based management consultancy I-Cubed, founded by two Black women.

Over 10,000 Black Britons from across the UK completed an extensive survey covering a range of social and cultural issues, from media and politics to mental health. Cambridge researchers also conducted dozens of in-depth interviews with a subset of participants.

Early interviews for the Black British Voices Project (BBVP) began in 2020, with a survey launching the following year. The findings have now been analysed in full and brought together in a major 104-page report, presented at a House of Commons event.

The report reveals that extremely high levels of distrust and discrimination are still felt deeply across Black British communities when it comes to systems such as health, education and criminal justice.

On education, 95% of respondents believe the UK's curriculum neglects Black lives and experiences, while fewer than 2% think educational institutions take racism seriously.

Some 87% expect to receive substandard levels of healthcare because of their race, while 79% believe the police still use stop and search unfairly against Black people.

'This report needs to start a conversation into the unequal outcomes that members of Black communities face in Britain,' said Dr Kenny Monrose, lead researcher and Cambridge sociologist.

'A lot of nonsense is talked about Black communities being hard to reach. They're not hard to reach, they're easy to ignore. But if there's 10,000 people speaking, attention needs to be paid. You might not want to agree, but you've got to listen to what's being said.'

The findings should be a 'wake-up call for Britain' argues Lester Holloway, Editor of The Voice. 'We have many fourth-generation Black Brits and, as a community, we should be feeling part of this country. Yet the lived experience of racism in every area of life is leading many to not feel British.'

British identity is highly divisive among Black communities. A majority (81%) describe themselves as British (either 'definitely' or 'somewhat'). The question of pride in Britain is split down the middle, with 49% of respondents proud to be British, while an almost equal number (45%) feel the opposite.

One participant described his British pride: 'I'm born here. I work here. I pay my taxes here. I bought my house here. Why should I not embrace it?' Others identify pride more locally, such as being a Londoner or NHS employee. However, many still see England's St. George's Cross flag as a threat.

'When I see the [St. George's Cross] hanging out the window, I'm crossing the road. I don't feel safe,' said one interviewee. 'I don't think they understand that to us it's a symbol of fear and racism.'

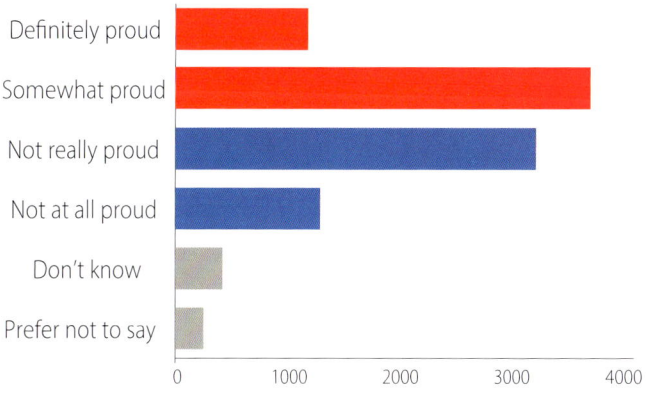

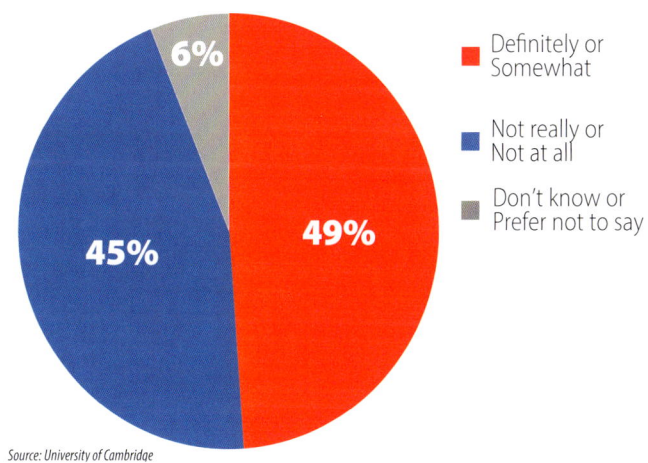

Source: University of Cambridge

The acronym 'BAME' (Black, Asian and Minority Ethnic) was considered 'unhelpfully homogenising' when classifying Britain's diverse non-White population, according to the report. Three-quarters (74%) of respondents felt uncomfortable with this label.

Faith matters more for Black communities than across the British population as a whole, with 84% of participants self-described as religious or spiritual (the 2021 census shows 56% of people in England and Wales identify with a religious faith).

When it comes to sexuality, a high number of respondents (84%) believe that Black LGBTQ+ people experience discrimination from within Black communities, although over half (56%) of BBVP participants say that acceptance of Black LGBTQ+ people has improved compared to a decade ago.

Interview data suggests there is still a fear of disclosing sexuality for many Black LGBTQ+ people, who worry about prejudice from church and family, as well as rejection from mainstream LGBTQ+ culture.

Along with widespread beliefs that UK education ignores Black experiences, and its institutions are unserious about racism, 41% of respondents 'definitely' believe discrimination to be the main barrier to academic attainment for young Black people.

Some interviewees discussed the importance of learning about histories of empire and slavery, while others pointed out the need to increase awareness of science and technology subjects in Black communities. Some 84% of BBVP participants felt that more Black teachers needed to be recruited.

'I'm disappointed to the point where it makes me slightly emotional… that more has not been done to encourage Black male teachers to go in to secondary schools,' said one interviewee. Another said that having a Black teacher meant '[y]ou don't have to prove that you're not a bad student.'

The workplace is perhaps where Black Britons most often experience individual racist behaviour as well as more indirect institutional prejudice, according to the report. Just 9% of respondents said they had little to no experience of workplace discrimination.

Interviewees spoke of a sense of pressure to justify their position, or feeling obliged to be the 'go-to person' in matters of race. Equality, Diversity, and Inclusion (EDI) workshops often led to discomfort, with one interviewee saying they are for 'White people to talk to other White people about race so they can tick a box…'

'Just because you've got diversity doesn't automatically mean you've got inclusion, and that's what's missing in these conversations,' said Monrose. BBVP respondents spoke of editing their names to assist pronunciation for co-workers, or altering clothing, hairstyles or speech patterns to 'fit in'.

Some 87% of survey participants said they have little to no trust in Britain's criminal justice system. Many comments focused on police behaviour that was felt to be unacceptable, yet tolerated by UK forces. A third of respondents say more Black officers would improve trust between police and Black communities, but a quarter think it unlikely even this would help much.

When asked about media representation, a huge 90% of respondents feel that advertising has improved over the last decade when it comes to portraying Black culture. However, over 93% also say that both Black men and women are negatively stereotyped by the media, film and television.

Do you think racial discrimination is the biggest barrier to young Black people's academic attainment?

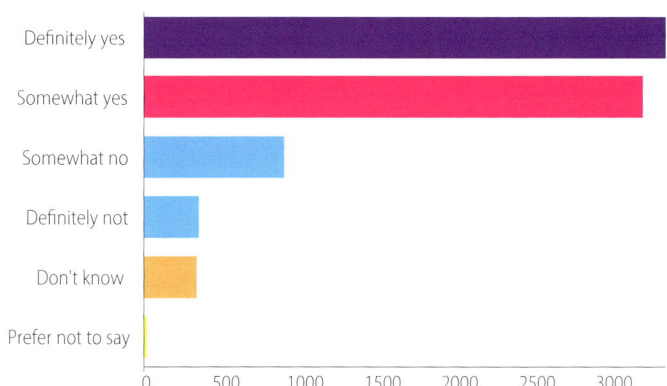

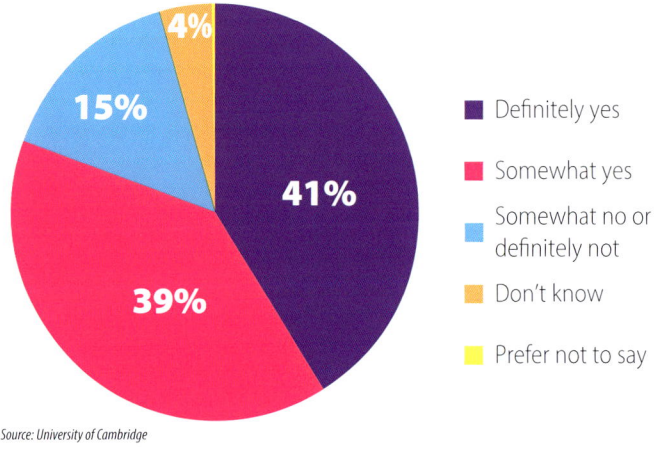

Source: University of Cambridge

Interviewees talked of frustration with depictions of Black people as 'victims rather than survivors'. Some pointed to double standards in media coverage of the personal lives of White and Black footballers. In fact, 63% of respondents felt that racism in sport has increased in recent years.

'Those taking the knee were booed by fans who then cheered Sterling when he scored a goal,' said one interviewee of an England football match, who described it as 'cognitive dissonance'.

Only 7% of research participants felt that Black people in Britain receive fair treatment from healthcare professionals.

The report highlights recent studies showing Black women were four times more likely than White women to die during childbirth.

Some 68% of respondents say they or a family member has suffered from mental health problems, and 87% say that Black families do not discuss mental health enough, including generational issues.

'There's some mental trauma that must've entailed growing up here as a Black man. The stories he tells…' said one interviewee of their father. Another participant described greater compassion shown to White prison inmates with psychiatric conditions than to Black inmates.

The report also explores Black people's attitudes to business and politics in the UK. A huge 95% of participants consider financial literacy 'critical' to more secure futures for Black Britons. The report argues that, for some, racial disparities in pay and pensions – combined with class hierarchies – create a 'fatalism' about economic fairness.

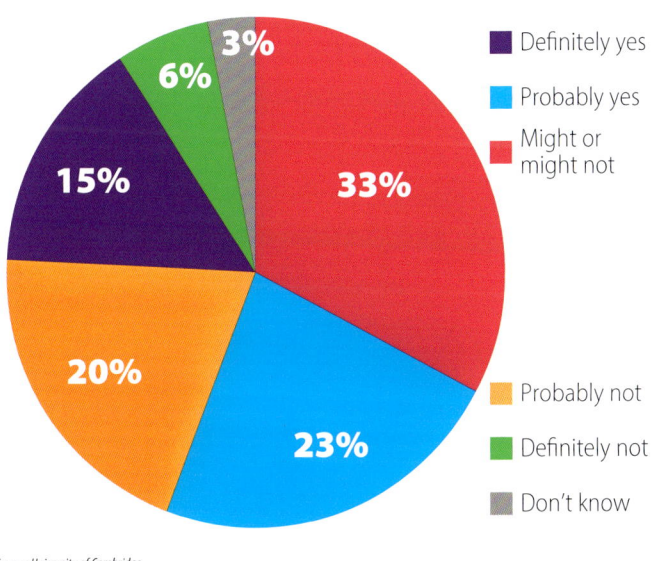

Would the recruitment of more Black police officers improve trust between the police and Black communities?

Source: University of Cambridge

Three out of four respondents expressed the view that Black businesses are treated unfairly by investors and financial institutions. Some interviewees argue that gentrification is pushing Black businesses out of their neighbourhoods in major cities.

Over 90% of all BBVP participants say they want to see more Black Members of Parliament. At a time of pervasive public cynicism about contemporary politics, an optimistic 22% also believe that Black politicians 'have the power to address the needs of Black people in Britain'.

The Johnson Government's 'Commission on Race and Ethnic Disparities' was singled out for criticism by a number of interviewees. 'For a man who referred to Black Lives Matter protesters as thugs… were we expecting anything else?' said one participant.

'We are mindful that historically black communities have been wary of reports conducted on race, as they attempt to limit or invalidate the reality of their lived experiences,' said Dr Monrose.

'However, the carpet of data captured within this report reliably highlights the chronic level of racial disparities and unequal outcomes that they face on a daily basis.'

Maya McFarlane, a Cambridge PhD candidate who worked on BBVP as an undergraduate and MPhil student, said she

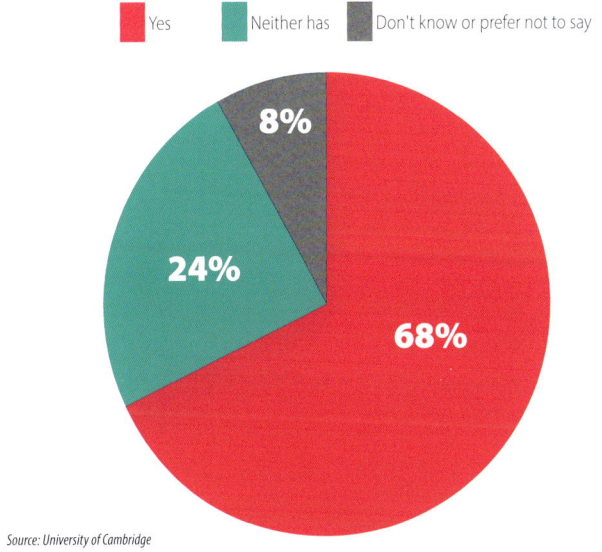

Have you or any members of your family suffered/or are suffering from mental health challenges?

Source: University of Cambridge

was 'immensely proud' to be part of the project.

'For centuries, sociological thought has been produced about Black people, but rarely has it been produced by us, or for our interests,' said McFarlane.

Dr Maggie Semple, OBE, co-founder of I-Cubed Consultancy, added: 'We can no longer overlook the lived realities of Black people in the UK and be non-committal in providing impactful long-term solutions.

'This is an opportunity to acknowledge our views and opinions, with the intent of creating a better future for us all.'

28 September 2023

The above information is reprinted with kind permission from the University of Cambridge.
© 2024 University of Cambridge
www.cam.ac.uk

Quarter of adults in England have negative view of those flying St George's cross

Labour voters take an especially negative view of the England flag.

By Matthew Smith, Head of Data Journalism

Today marks St George's Day, and the red cross of St George will be flying all over the country. The flag of England has been at the centre of several rows in recent years, and now a new YouGov survey examines attitudes towards the act of flying the flag.

Most Britons (57%) say they have a favourable opinion of people flying the England flag outside their home, including 61% of adults in England. However, a quarter (27%) say they have an unfavourable opinion, including 24% among adults in England.

These results are similar to our previous survey in 2018, which found that 56% of Britons had a favourable view of those flying the England flag, and 24% a negative one. (The results among English adults specifically are likewise almost identical.)

Disapproval of the England flag is not unique, however, being slightly higher than the 18–22% who have an unfavourable view of those flying the UK, Scottish and Welsh flags. Indeed, approximately 13% of Britons expressed a negative attitude towards flying ALL flags listed.

Attitudes towards the flags are political in nature, particularly when it comes to the English flag. Fully 44% of 2019 Labour voters in Britain have a negative view of those who fly the England flag – higher than the 37% who have a favourable view – these figures are virtually identical among Labour voters in England specifically. By contrast, only 10% of 2019 Tories in Britain have a negative view of England flag-flyers.

English 2019 Labour voters are notably more negative towards the England and Union flags than they are towards

Source: YouGov

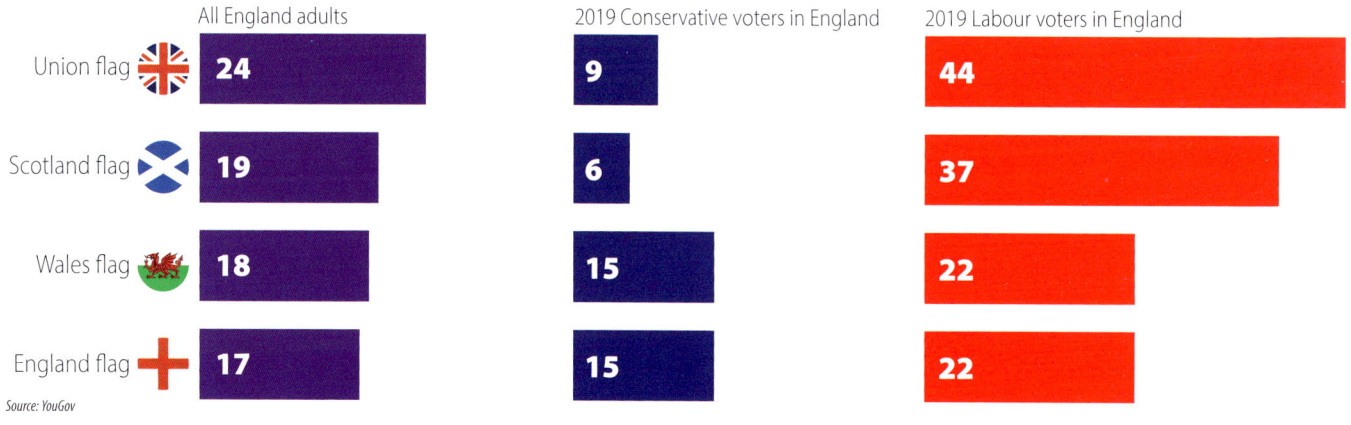

Source: YouGov

Negativity among the Scottish and Welsh towards the England flag is not reciprocated by the English

Do you have a favourable or unfavourable opinion of people flying or displaying each of the following types of flag at their home?
% of 2,004 GB adults, including 1,707 adults in England, 188 adults in Scotland, and 109 adults in Wales

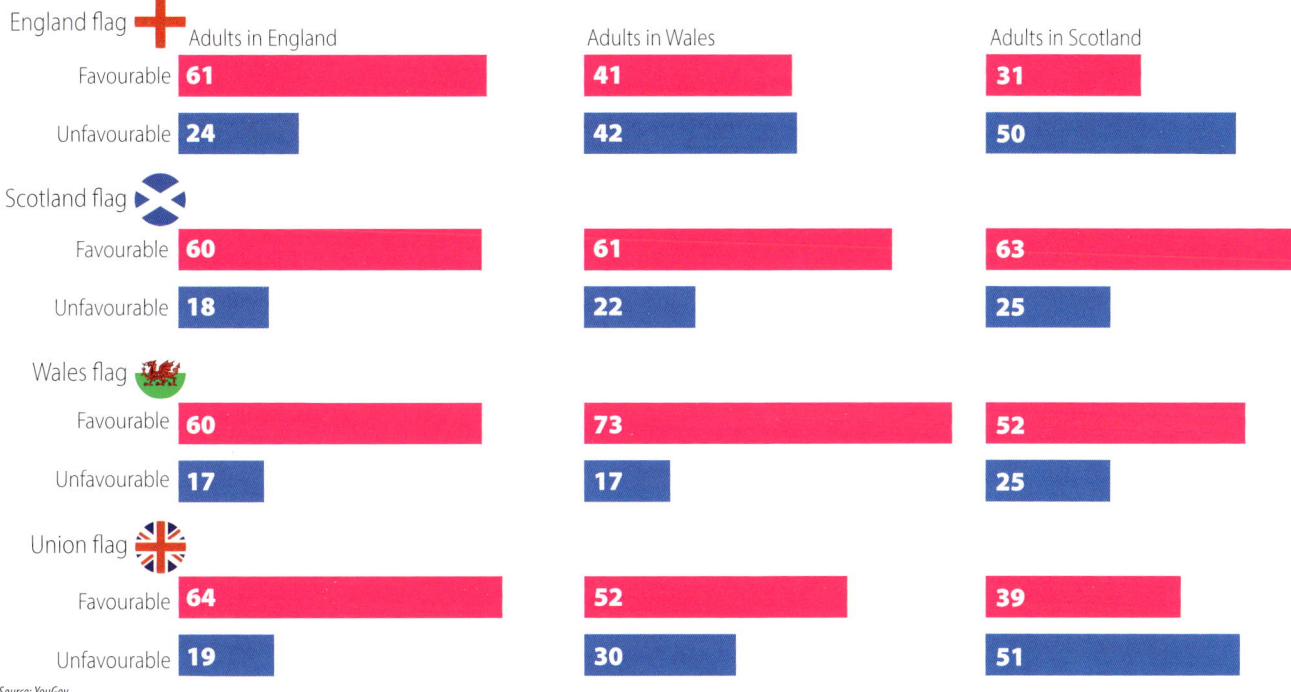

Source: YouGov

St George is cross: adults in England say that the depiction of the flag on the men's football kit is unacceptable

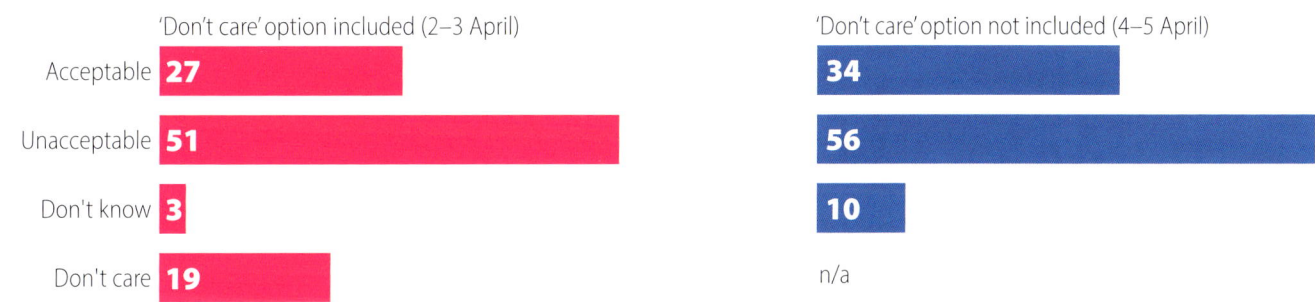

Source: YouGov

the Scottish and Welsh flags – while the aforementioned 44% dislike flying the England flag and 37% the Union flag, this falls to 22% for the Scottish and Welsh flags.

Perhaps unsurprisingly, Scots tend to have a negative view of those who fly the England flag (50%, versus 31% who have a favourable opinion), while in Wales people are split 41% to 42%.

There is no such reciprocal disdain among the English for those flying Scottish or Welsh flags – 60% of English people have a favourable opinion in both cases.

Flags on sports kits

March saw a row over Nike's 'playful update' of the England flag on the men's team's kit ahead of the 2024 Euros, with Rishi Sunak and Keir Starmer the addition of blue and purple stripes to the design.

Curious as it might have appeared for the prime minister and leader of the opposition to weigh in on the debate, their views reflect those of the wider population – 56% of adults in England say that it is unacceptable to depict the England flag in this way. Only a third consider it acceptable (34%).

A version of the England flag question asked a couple of days earlier included an option for respondents to say they 'don't care' about the England flag depiction issue. Providing this option saw 19% express their disinterest, seemingly drawing from all points of view: compared to the question without a don't care option, the effect was to reduce 'acceptable' responses by seven points, 'unacceptable' by five points, and 'don't know' by seven points.

At around the same time a media storm also brewed over a redesigned Union Jack as merchandise for Team GB.

On this concept the public are split – 47% of Britons thought the Team GB fan flag was acceptable and 46% did not.

23 April 2024

The above information is reprinted with kind permission from YouGov.
© 2024 YouGov PLC

www.yougov.co.uk

Is the England flag racist?

The flag of England, known as the St George's Cross, is a simple red cross on a white background. It's been a symbol of England for centuries, but in recent years, some have raised concerns that it's being misused in ways that could be seen as raciSt Let's explore the history of the flag, why some people feel uncomfortable about it, and how it can be reclaimed as a symbol for everyone in England.

A brief history of the St George's Cross

The St George's Cross has been associated with England since the Middle Ages. St George, the flag's namesake, was a Roman soldier and Christian martyr who is believed to have lived in the 3rd century. Legend says he slayed a dragon, which has made him a symbol of bravery and protection. His cross, a red one on a white background, became England's flag around the 13th century.

The flag was used by English soldiers during the Crusades, and by the 1500s, it was flying on ships and buildings across the country. Over time, the St George's Cross became firmly linked to England's national identity.

How is the England flag seen today?

There are four countries in the United Kingdom (UK): England, Scotland, Wales, and Northern Ireland. Each has its own flag. Scotland has the white diagonal cross of St Andrew on a blue background. Wales uses a dragon, and Northern Ireland's flag is a red cross with a crown and star. The Union Jack, which combines the crosses of England, Scotland, and Ireland, represents the entire UK.

Unlike the Union Jack, the St George's Cross is specifically English, and over the years, it has sometimes been associated with negative ideas. Some people, especially those from ethnic minority backgrounds, feel the flag has been used by far-right groups who promote racist or xenophobic views. These groups may wave the flag while claiming their views represent 'real' Englishness, which can make others feel unwelcome or excluded.

Misuse of the flag by extremist groups

Some far-right nationalist groups have adopted the St George's Cross as a symbol of their anti-immigrant or anti-foreigner agendas. When these groups misuse the flag to represent hatred, it creates a negative association with the symbol, making it seem racist or unwelcoming.

However, it's important to remember that these groups don't own the flag. Their views do not represent the vast majority of people in England, who see the flag simply as a representation of their country, culture, and history.

How can the St George's Cross be reclaimed?

To reclaim the flag, it needs to be used in ways that promote inclusivity and pride for all people who call England home, regardless of their background. People from all races, religions, and cultures who are proud to be English should feel comfortable waving the St George's Cross.

Celebrating the flag during sporting events, cultural festivals, and national holidays helps emphasise that it belongs to everyone in England, not just one group. When people from diverse communities use the flag to express their love for the country, it sends a strong message that being English isn't tied to any one race or identity.

Schools and communities can play a big role by educating young people about the history of the flag and how it can be a positive symbol of unity. It's also important to call out and reject any hate or racism that's linked to the flag. By using the St George's Cross in a positive, inclusive way, we can reclaim it as a symbol that represents the best of England: a country of diversity, tolerance, and unity.

In conclusion, while some may misuse the England flag for negative purposes, it's not inherently raciSt By promoting inclusivity and celebrating the flag's true meaning, it can be a positive symbol for all who live in England.

I knew what it was like being black and British – but when I moved to the US, I was called the N-word for the first time

As I walk around my campus, I now wonder: what does it mean for me to be standing on ground built by slaves?

By June Eric-Udorie

I don't know when I started feeling so much terror when I saw a US police officer. My heart races and my hands get clammy whenever I walk past them. Whenever they greet me, I make sure to respond quickly, with an additional 'sir' or 'ma'am' at the end to signify respect.

This is not to say that police officers didn't sometimes make me uneasy in my hometown of London. Earlier this year, data showed that police are four times more likely to use force against black people than white people in London, despite black people accounting for only 13% of London's population.

But here, it's slightly different. This is the American South, after all. I sometimes wonder: what would happen if I was rude to an officer, or if I didn't return their greeting? Would the officer shoot me for being aggressive? Or would that be the excuse that he would use?

This scenario plays over and over in my head as I struggle to come to terms with what it means to be black in America, scared that one wrong move could lead to me being dead in seconds.

Last August, I moved to Durham, North Carolina to attend Duke University. I came knowing that even though I'd experienced racism in the UK – being asked, 'Where are you really from?' at school; being told to 'go back to where you really come from' after Brexit; and being followed around by staff at my local Marks & Spencer – that it would be difficult to adjust to America's racism.

It was here that two students called me a 'n*****r' at 2am; here where a friend taught me to make sure the police knew where my hands were; here that a black cashier at the supermarket shared with me her fears that one day her son will not return home.

I don't tell these stories to dismiss the racism that black people and minority ethnic individuals face in the UK. But rather, I am meditating on how I adjust to the way race and racism functions in the US, and how it is built into the fabric of our society in the UK.

When I contemplate what it means to be a queer black woman in the American South, it feels heavy. It's not dissimilar – just somewhat familiar. Just like in the UK, I am aware that white people's racism can determine the outcome of my future. But I still don't know how to understand that a police officer, or a white supremacist, could see me and shoot, and that would be the end.

I'm dealing with the immediate legacy of slavery, which I see every day in deeply segregated cities and schools, and how that racial schema produced a hierarchical arrangement that we don't discuss enough. As I walk around my campus, I wonder: what does it mean for me, as a black woman, to be standing on ground built by slaves? What does it mean to be celebrating 50 years of black students studying at an institution that has existed for centuries?

How should I process the fact that my university only just recognised that an African American designed the school's main campus?

Yes, the racism here is everywhere and violent, but the longer I stay here, the more I realise that it is the same.

In the UK, we're really good at erasing the legacies of slavery and colonialism, and how so many of us are still carrying that trauma. But being in the American South has forced me to contend with what was sometimes easier to ignore about race and racism in the UK.

Black people dying in police custody. Black boys being stopped and searched. Black women being killed by the police. Black children being failed by their schools. In short, the racism in the UK is just as insidious and violent as the racism I'm learning to live with in the US. The problem is that it's so easy to point to America's killings of black people, to say 'that's not happening here' and to ignore everything else. There are many ways in which the state is slowly killing black people, and just because it doesn't come in the form of a gunshot doesn't mean it doesn't matter.

I don't think I'll ever forget being called a 'n****r.' I don't think I'll ever stop feeling terrified around the police. But being in the American South for the last 12 months has forced me to realise just how global anti-blackness is, and just how far we have to go.

1 September 2021

The above information is reprinted with kind permission from *The Independent*.
© independent.co.uk 2024

www.independent.co.uk

The 'anti-racists' want me to hate Britain

This country is one of the most tolerant in the world. But there is a limit to how much a society can take before it breaks.

By Dia Chakravarty

Nobody divides us more than the so-called 'anti-racists'. And the damage they are doing to our society, I fear, will soon become irreparable.

Barely a week goes by without another self-appointed, self-anointed do-gooder telling me that I should feel unwelcome in my country. This week, I found out from a new report that the British countryside is 'racist' and 'colonial', governed by 'white British cultural values', and that the perception that the countryside is a 'white space' prevents people like me from enjoying the outdoors.

Racist, colonial, white (only ever in an accusatory sense) – these terms have been so persistently and meticulously injected into every aspect of our public life that we no longer bat an eyelid when we come across a paragraph like the one above in an apparently serious document, intended to inform policy. But what does any of it mean?

With which 'ethnic minority values' would the taxpayer-funded charities, who backed the report, like to replace the offending 'white values' when it comes to the enjoyment of the countryside? Why is British culture not considered to be something for all of us Brits to embrace, irrespective of race or religion? What makes it a 'white' culture that is apparently being imposed on the rest of us?

If there were to be identifiably separate ethnic minority values, would my Bangladeshi values be more acceptable to a Nigerian Brit, purely because they would be untainted by 'whiteness'? If not, then how are these distinct values meant to operate within the same space without impinging on each other? Does the absurdity of these ideas really need to be spelt out?

It is truly astonishing that a report can get away with this insidious sentence: 'The perception that green spaces are dominated by white people can prevent people from ethnic minority backgrounds from using green spaces.' But white people are the largest ethnic group in England and Wales, forming 82% of the population. According to this report, ethnic minorities are uncomfortable sharing a space with the dominant ethnic group in the country.

Do the authors feel that people like me are generally unhappy in a white majority country? What exactly is the white population meant to do about this perceived problem? It beggars belief that this sort of divisive, dehumanising and dangerous thinking is what counts as inclusivity in the West today.

This has got to stop. This constant drip feed of the sinister narrative of white versus non-whites, the oppressors versus the oppressed is guaranteed to lead the nation down a path of social strife of the kind we read about in countries far away.

Britain is one of the most tolerant countries in the world and Brits among the most tolerant of peoples. But there is a limit to how far any society can be pushed before it breaks. Continue to tell the indigenous population that their culture, their lifestyle, their very existence is a threat and an affront to their ethnic minority fellow countrymen and there will come a time when the resentment will become so great that the resulting backlash will be extremely difficult to control or contain.

It is tempting to dismiss all this as fear-mongering, particularly for those who have never lived in a less stable country. But for those of us who have made a home here, after leaving a tumultuous past behind, these concerns are very real.

9 February 2024

The above information is reprinted with kind permission from *The Telegraph*.
© Telegraph Media Group Limited 2024

www.telegraph.co.uk

The delusion of racial tolerance in the UK

By David Roberts

'The greatest trick the devil ever played, was making us believe he doesn't exist

The Usual Suspect

A very British notion

Britain has long prided itself on being a tolerant society. Far Right rags like *The Spectator* proudly trumpet Britain's 'tolerance' in the face of a 'few football racists' that can be dismissed as rotten apples. Diversity UK pointed out that 'seventy years ago in Britain, issues of race and identity were unfamiliar to most [if you were White]. However, since then the face of the nation has changed rapidly'. The education group 'Total People' claims tolerance is a primary value in the UK.

Britain's reward for such tolerance is to be perceived as 'morally praiseworthy'. But what is it being praised for? Polycarp Ikuenobe argues that this reward is in fact about restraint: it is about 'refraining from mistreating others regarding their racial difference'. It shows that there is a power dynamic at work in the act of tolerating someone else. There is an implied right NOT to tolerate under certain conditions decided by those professing tolerance. Magali Bessone describes the act of tolerance as 'Refraining from interfering with something deeply disapproved of in spite of having the power to interfere.'

Here is the power we rarely consider: tolerance condones judgmental interference by the judging, dominant, and powerful. Power is present in both interference and in not interfering. It is masked by the concept's rhetorical magnanimity. The relationship between those expressing tolerance, and those they are judging, is asymmetrical.

Where occasional intolerance arises, like at those 'few football matches' *The Spectator* pointed at, they are reduced to individual acts, every time they happen, no matter how many times they happen. They are separated from cause and effect relationships, disconnected from any organised determinism that might intrude on the sanctity of the idea of 'tolerance'. Where that fails, such acts' connections to organisation are cloaked in misdirection, misrepresentation, lies and obfuscation, all to protect the myth that organised racism doesn't exist.

But there's no shortage of examples of majority behaviour being misrepresented as an unhinged, illegitimate minority when in fact, support for such racism is widespread. Think Brexit; racism remarketed as patriotism. Think Meghan; the idea of a woman of Colour 'polluting' a blue blood, White-skinned hereditary monarchy that is itself a hundred shades of European that Brexiteers ran from. Or the brutal, racist bile that poured into the Twittersphere and wider media from old, racist, white misogynist men openly using Far Right 'news' platforms to actively, publicly, unashamedly incite racial hatred, telling people to throw excrement at a woman of Colour who has 'infected' the imperial Royal Family in the UK. Think millions applauding an imperial monarch and her reign over the world, and the preservation of the last vestiges of formal empire in the shape of the Commonwealth. These are instead all unrelated acts, for the Right, who refuse to see cause and effect in anything they are responsible for.

Think of the dreadful racism directed at Marcus Rashford and two others after England lost at the EUFA Euro 2020; just the odd idiot on Twitter, or a residue of race hatred that, despite a self-proclaiming 'tolerant' society, is an immutable, violent, painful, oppressive constant?

The claim to tolerance masks and denies the notion, the intolerable, horrible idea, that all those individual acts might form part of a larger structure, a learned – and therefore taught – code of behaviour, a pan-national attitude of hostility or disdain or hatred or fear. The UK Court system is acknowledging institutional racism. The British healthcare system is now found to harbour institutional racism. UK mental healthcare is similarly afflicted. The police are also concerned about their own racist structures, and an independent review of the Fire Brigade found it to be institutionally racist and misogynist. Its author warned this would be a common theme across UK public services. The former Vice-Chancellor of Loughborough University openly recognised institutional racism at the university in an interview with alumnus Mike Wedderburn, the sports commentator. Another Vice-Chancellor declared it a problem across the whole sector. Britain's national identity, pride and progress were made on Empire, as so many nationalists never tire of pointing out. It should be no surprise that imperial attitudes, of racial superiority, remain deeply embedded in all aspects of government, its institutions and their instructions to society.

Are we actually tolerant of intolerance?

So we are left in a quandary: if we are tolerant of race, why is there racism everywhere, every day? Perhaps some answers lie in the idea of the term itself. What does it involve? How might you feel, if you were told that someone tolerated you? Where is power revealed to lie? With you or with them? I feel dominated and patronised when I think of that dynamic. I feel like a child whose existence is accepted on condition of not upsetting anyone – seen and not heard, permitted as long as I concord with certain conditions of my existence that have been set by someone else, by the society in which I am permitted to reside. Tolerance involves degrees of resistance: I accept you here but do not necessarily wish you here. Your presence is not at my request but I will accept it as long as it breaks no rules or challenges my right to determine how or to what extent I accept you. Tolerance is power.

Tolerance has been defined as 'value orientation towards difference'. Value orientation encompasses the ensemble of convictions, attitudes, behaviours that are in a hierarchical relationship and monitored by values in a social environment.

Among other things, this means there is a sector of society whose values are considered legitimate and dominant, passing judgment on another group of people whose values may be different, or appear different, or intimidate because of that perceived difference. Tolerance in this form is a toxic structure and process because it masks the same power relationship that its use implies does not exist – the devil's greatest trick.

British values about racial groups have historically been linked to its imperial history: that period of global dominance without which the UK would not have industrialised and evolved into a global superpower of the 20th century. The country's economic descent and its collapse in comparative global prowess over recent decades does not detract from what placed it at its apogee until its place in the world was challenged by newer superpowers. Britain once controlled nearly one quarter of all people on the planet, through an empire over which the sun never set. This was then, and, for almost half the population, still is, a source of great national pride in a halcyonic era that many continue to believe defines the best of Britain.

Since Empire is always based on superiority, whether Roman, Nazi or British, the dynamic of White and Black mirrors that eugenicist ideology. Empires stole countries and then tolerated the presence of their indigenous populations (Cesaire, 1972; Fanon, 1961; Mbembe, 2020). Those indigenes who served imperial occupation were tolerated as long as they did not contravene the interests of the colonisers. Permissions were granted for integration within the colonial institutions on condition of loyal subservience. Our presence in our own lands was tolerated as long as we didn't get 'uppity'. Those subjects of Empire who were admitted to the White Motherland required similar permissions and tolerances, and still require permission to stay, after decades of residence, in the face of ignorant, racist, State persecution. In the face of tolerance.

Tolerance involves the power to grant permissions to others with less power. In this case, it is White England granting terms of existence to those of Colour who are literal and figurative descendants of Windrush. White England is a concept. It is made up of government elites, Left and Right, who set the tone of race relations through the Executive and Legislature (the contemporary Right in the West is almost always far more racist than the Left). It is the courts that apply the laws of the land. It is the police who execute them. It is the media that reports according to its ideological and racist biases. It is the wider society that watches such procedure and takes its cue from those rulers and rules and permissions and exclusions and constraints and limits; and takes its cue from that tolerance of the Other as determined by imperial history and political identity. Power is present in both interference and in not interfering, but it is masked by the label's rhetorical magnanimity. The greatest trick…

In the end…

Tolerance permits difference as long as the difference doesn't get 'uppity'. And as long as 'tolerant racism' is the mindset of a society and its institutions, that mindset will reinforce racism, and restrict change to the terms and conditions of White Fragility. This term refers to 'a state in which even a minimum amount of racial stress becomes intolerable, triggering a range of defensive moves' like denial, misdirection, misrepresentation, obfuscation, lies and so on. In Derrick Bell's words, tolerance will be framed by interest divergence: People of Colour in the UK, under a regime of 'tolerance', can co-exist as long as what they do does not clash with what White England wants to happen. Thereafter, 'tolerance' becomes 'intolerance'; but tolerance is already intolerant. It comes from and perpetuates racial power, control and abuse, whilst presenting as doing the opposite. 'Tolerance' is the 'credible' institutional face of race relations in the UK; we pride ourselves on this Janus term. Making us believe…

As long as we can claim to be tolerant, we have done nothing wrong and nothing needs to change. Yet for many People of Colour, tolerance is imperial continuity; the past in the present, as Mbembe said. Tolerance is a mindset rooted in relations of power that ceded and cede limited freedoms to a captured society. That mindset is masturbatory self-indulgence and denial that we still use to congratulate ourselves on our sterling contribution to race relations. We are not who we think we are, in the same way that America is not the land of the free or the home of the brave. Those who have exercised racial violence most, are those most active in denying it, and defending and disguising the ideology it rests on. As George Orwell wrote in *The Road to Wigan Pier*, people tend to think they can 'abolish [societal] distinctions without making any uncomfortable change in their own habits and ideology'. They cannot. Until British people move away from a nationalist mindset that internalises and sanctions permission granting by a dominant race over a subjugated Other as a way of being multicultural, we will remain in race purgatory, with the Devil looking on.

26 November 2022

The above information is reprinted with kind permission from David Roberts.
© David Roberts 2024

www.davidrobertsonline.org

Over a third of people from minority groups have experienced racist assaults, survey finds

By Joe Stafford

More than a third of people from ethnic and religious minority groups in Britain have experienced some form of racist assault, according to new research led by experts from The University of Manchester, the University of St Andrews and King's College London.

The Evidence for Equality National Survey (EVENS) is a major new survey of racism and ethnic inequalities carried out by the Centre on the Dynamics of Ethnicity (CoDE), which reveals the extent of racism and racial discrimination experienced by people from ethnic and religious minority groups.

The racism reported by the survey's respondents took different forms – physical, verbal or damage to property – and happened in all areas of life including education, work and when looking for housing.

Overall, almost one in six respondents had experienced a racially motivated physical assault, but over a third of people identifying as Gypsy/Traveller, Roma or Other Black reported that they had been physically assaulted because of their ethnicity, race, colour, or religion.

Over a quarter had been verbally abused or insulted because of their ethnicity, race, colour, or religion, and 17% reported experiencing damage to their personal property. Nearly a third reported racial discrimination in education and employment, and nearly a fifth reported racial discrimination when looking for housing.

Racial discrimination in education was reported by around half of those who identified as Roma, Any Other Black, Black Caribbean and Mixed White and Caribbean, with 44% of Gypsy/Traveller respondents saying the same. Some ethnic groups also reported high rates of discrimination from the police, including over a third of people from the Black Caribbean, Any Other Black, Roma and Gypsy/Traveller groups.

People from ethnic minority groups are subjected to racial discrimination from their neighbours and while going about their everyday lives. Between 40–50% of people from Black Caribbean, Any Other Black, and White and Black Caribbean groups reported facing racist abuse while out shopping, in parks, cafes or restaurants or on public transport. Almost one in six people also experienced racial discrimination from their neighbours, but this rose to one in two Other Black people and one in three Gypsy/Traveller people.

During the first year of the Covid-19 pandemic, Chinese, Other Asian and Eastern European people reported an increase in experiences of racial discrimination relative to other ethnic minority groups, and some ethnic groups reported increased policing during the first year of the pandemic – one in three Gypsy/Traveller people, and one in five Roma and Chinese people had been stopped by the police in this period.

'Our data is stark evidence that racism is an enduring feature of British society today. However, tackling racism is not just a case of merely removing "bad apples" from workplaces and institutions such as the Metropolitan Police – We need to seriously transform the policies and procedures that enable racist discrimination to persist, in order to ensure better outcome and life chances for ethnic and religious minority people.' – Dr Dharmi Kapadia, Senior Lecturer in Sociology at The University of Manchester

'The EVENS survey allows us to obtain a deeper understanding of the insidiousness and persistence of racial discrimination in the UK,' said Professor Laia Bécares, Professor of Social Science and Health at King's College London. 'We clearly document that there is a high level of racism in the UK which permeates all aspects of people's everyday lives and impacts their health, wellbeing, and socioeconomic circumstances.'

'The innovative, robust survey techniques we used mean we have a larger dataset and detailed data on more ethnic and religious minority groups across a wider range of topics than ever before,' said Professor Nissa Finney, Professor of Human Geography at the University of St Andrews. 'This makes our data a powerful tool for understanding, and reducing, ethnic and religious inequalities.'

'It can be easy to look back on the violent, explicit racism of earlier decades and think that racial discrimination is not a major problem in Britain today, but our data proves this idea wrong,' said Professor James Nazroo, Professor of Sociology at The University of Manchester. 'Now we have this evidence, it is simply not acceptable to pretend racism does not exist and to carry on as before – EVENS is a wake-up call to make society fairer for everybody.'

19 April 2023

The above information is reprinted with kind permission from The University of Manchester.
© 2024 The University of Manchester
www.manchester.ac.uk

Enough is enough: calling an end to racist points-scoring

An election year is the ideal time to address anti-Gypsy, Roma and Traveller rhetoric, says Yvonne MacNamara.

In this super-election year, as political parties gear up for campaigns and strategise their platforms, there's one issue that cannot be swept under the rug any longer: the pervasive racism faced by Romani (Gypsy), Roma and Irish Traveller communities across Britain.

Discrimination against these communities is as common as rain, yet it seems to be conveniently overlooked or exploited for political gain. This year we say enough is enough.

In the same week the former Labour Party candidates for Rochdale and Hyndburn were rightfully dropped for anti-Semitism, another story broke highlighting the deep-rooted racism that pervades our society.

The Equalities and Human Rights Commission served Pontins with an unlawful act notice after an investigation by the equality watchdog found multiple instances of race discrimination against Irish Travellers.

The day before we wrote to the leader of the Labour Party Sir Keir Starmer calling for immediate action to be taken over a racist slur previously posted online by the Labour candidate for North East mayor Kim McGuinness ('f*** off, I'm not a gypsy'). So what does Pontins have to do with party politics? Everything.

When the Pontins story broke we saw no solidarity from any of the major political parties, no statements on the dire racist practices that had gone on at the holiday camp. Because political parties are scared to stand up for our communities.

Every time there is an election coming up we receive reports of racist rhetoric used by candidates in their literature and flashy campaign videos to win votes.

Recently the Conservative MP for Bournemouth West put out an appeal to his electorate to oppose a proposed new settled site because he said Travellers didn't belong in a 'residential area.' The racist dog whistling is used to play on the racist rhetoric towards Gypsy, Roma and Irish Traveller people that has been pervasive in Europe for centuries.

Gypsy, Roma and Irish Travellers have fallen victim to state oppression for centuries. There was the 'Tinker experiment' from 1940 to 1980 in Scotland that sought to take children from their families and put them into residential homes to 'knock the Tinker out of the child'; the forced enslavement of Roma for five centuries in central Europe; and the murder of Roma in their hundreds of thousands by the Nazi regime in the Holocaust. Racism towards these communities is very real and it is very violent.

When politicians fail to tackle racism towards Gypsy, Roma and Irish Travellers they give a green light to Pontins, Butlins and Wetherspoon to refuse service. When parties fail to act they tell the overzealous police officer there is nothing wrong with racially profiling a young Traveller. When politicians fail to drive out racism in their own parties they are complicit in that racism.

Pontins is a victory for racial justice, and we are glad our hard work to bring this story into the light has resulted in action from the EHRC. But this case is one in a long line of organisations being pulled up for racist practices and we still see new cases every day.

Currently the EHRC is stuck between a rock and a hard place, underfunded by central government and fearful of upsetting them in case of retribution. A truly independent EHRC would have the ability to pursue larger cases and get to the heart of tackling discrimination and racism.

In this election year we need a decisive commitment to end the direct and institutional racism towards our communities from across the political spectrum. This starts with reforms to the EHRC so it has the powers to effectively enforce anti-racist legislation, but ultimately rests on parties to call out the racism in their ranks for what it is. If not now then when?

22 February 2024

The above information is reprinted with kind permission from *The Morning Star*.
© 2024 The People's Press Printing Society

www.morningstaronline.co.uk

'Pervasive and relentless' racism on the rise in Europe, survey finds

Poll of 6,752 people of African descent in 13 countries finds almost half have experienced discrimination.

By Daniel Boffey, Chief reporter

Racism is 'pervasive and relentless' and on the rise in Europe, with nearly half of black people in member states surveyed by the EU reporting discrimination, from the verbal abuse of their children to being blocked by landlords from renting homes.

In every walk of life, from schools to the job market, housing and health, a survey by the EU's rights agency of people of African descent found high levels of discrimination, with some of the worst results recorded in Austria and Germany, where far-right parties have been on the rise.

The survey of 6,752 people of African descent in 13 countries – Austria, Belgium, Denmark, Finland, France, Germany, Ireland, Italy, Luxembourg, Poland, Portugal, Spain and Sweden – found 45% had experienced racial discrimination, an increase of six percentage points from 39% in 2016.

In Austria and Germany, three in four of those questioned (72% and 76%) said they had felt discriminated against in the last five years, up from a half (51% and 52%) when the same question was asked in 2016.

The anti-immigration Alternative für Deutschland became the third-largest party in Germany, as well as the largest opposition, after the federal elections of 2017. They did less well in 2021 but their influence is growing.

An AfD politician was elected to the post of district administrator, the equivalent of a mayor, in Germany for the first time in June, with more recent electoral triumphs in the west of the country leading it to describe itself as a 'major all-German party'.

In Austria, the Freedom party (FPÖ), founded in 1956 and first led by a former Nazi functionary and SS officer, is leading in the polls ahead of a general election next year, which it is expected to win.

Michael O'Flaherty, director at the EU's fundamental rights agency, which advises the European Commission on policy, said the results in the report, Being Black in the EU, were 'shameful'.

He called for all EU countries to gather equality data, including on ethnic or racial origin, in an attempt to further grip the problem. Owing to sensitivities arising from the Second World War, Germany, unlike the UK, does not collect census data on racial or ethnic diversity.

O'Flaherty said: 'It is shocking to see no improvement since our last survey in 2016. Instead, people of African descent face ever more discrimination just because of the colour of their skin.

'Racism and discrimination should have no place in our societies. The EU and its member states should use these findings to better target their efforts and ensure people of African descent, too, can enjoy their rights freely without racism and discrimination,' he said.

The racism uncovered by the agency was said to affect people's daily lives. One in four (23%) respondents said that a private property owner had prevented them from renting a home because of their racial or ethnic origin.

A quarter (23%) of black people indicated that someone made offensive or threatening comments to their child in person because of their ethnic or immigrant background. Almost two out of five parents in Ireland (39%), Germany and Finland (both 38%) and Austria (37%) reported such experiences.

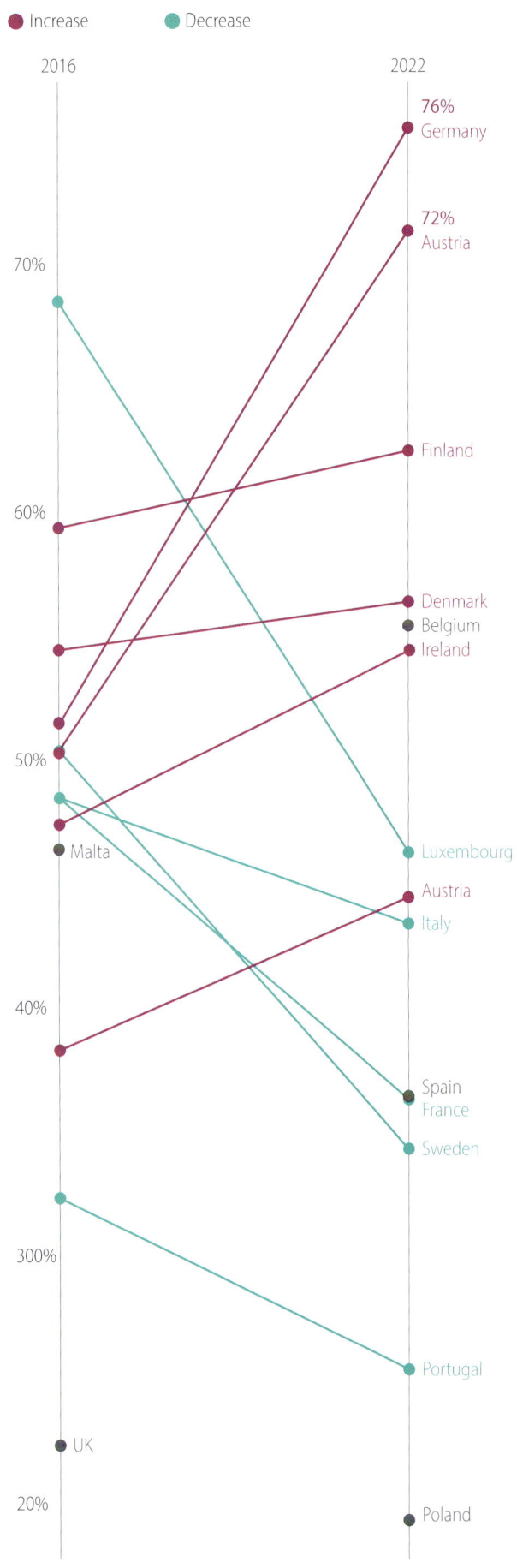

Prevalence of racial discrimination
% of respondents of African descent who experienced discrimination in the 5 years before survey

Source: Being Black in the EU, experiences of people of African descent. European Union Agency for Fundamental Rights, 2023.
Note: All respondents who had engaged in activities related to work, education, public services and commercial spaces detailed in the survey.

Across the countries surveyed, young people of African descent were found to be three times more likely to leave school early, compared with the general population.

One in four (26%) of respondents said they had been stopped by the police in the five years before the survey. Among those, about half (48%) characterised the most recent stop as racial profiling.

The average proportion of black people who said they believed they had been a victim of ethnic profiling by the police had increased across the countries surveyed from 41% in 2016 to 48% in 2022, when the latest survey was undertaken.

On average, the employment rate among people of African descent aged 20 to 64 years (71%) was found to be similar to that of the general population (73%) of the same age range. But almost a third (32%) of respondents were working in 'elementary occupations', compared with an average of 8% for the general population across all 27 EU member states.

Almost a third (30%) of employed people of African descent have a temporary contract. This proportion was said to be three times that of the general population across the EU (11%). Black people were also found to be disproportionately over-qualified for the jobs in which they were working. A third (35%) of black people with university-level qualifications were found to be in low or medium skilled occupations compared with 21% for the general population.

Respondents to the EU survey were either born in countries of sub-Saharan Africa or were descendants of immigrants with at least one parent born in sub-Saharan Africa.

25 October 2023

Key facts

- In Austria and Germany, three in four people of African descent said they had felt discriminated against in the last five years.
- One in four people of African descent said that a private property owner had prevented them from renting a home because of their racial or ethnic origin.
- A quarter of black people indicated that someone made offensive or threatening comments to their child in person because of their ethnic or immigrant background.

The above information is reprinted with kind permission from *The Guardian*.
© 2024 Guardian News and Media Limited

www.theguardian.com

Fighting Racism

Chapter 3

Turning awareness into action: how you can challenge racism

Imagine walking into school and overhearing someone making a hurtful comment based on someone's race. It's an unsettling feeling, isn't it? This is a daily reality for some, but it doesn't have to be. Racism, in its many forms, affects individuals and communities deeply, but each of us has the power to make a change. By confronting these issues directly, we can create a society that values fairness and inclusivity.

10 Ways to challenge racism

1. Educate yourself and others

Knowledge is power. The more you understand about different cultures and the history of racism, the better equipped you'll be to identify and challenge racial prejudices. Hosting book clubs, sharing articles, and watching documentaries on these topics can broaden perspectives within your community.

2. Speak up in the moment

Silence can be seen as approval. When witnessing racist actions or comments, calmly and firmly express why the behaviour or speech is unacceptable. This might feel intimidating but can lead to important conversations and change.

3. Support diverse businesses

Put your money where your mouth is. Supporting businesses owned by individuals from diverse racial backgrounds can boost economic equality and foster community solidarity.

4. Promote inclusive practices at school

Work with school administrations to ensure the curriculum and school activities include diverse perspectives. This helps create an educational environment where all students feel represented and valued.

5. Use social media for good

Harness the power of your online platforms to advocate for racial equality. Share information, challenge misconceptions, and promote narratives from people of colour.

6. Participate in community dialogues

Join or organise forums where people from different backgrounds can discuss experiences and ideas for tackling racial injustice. These dialogues can be pivotal in transforming community perspectives.

7. Volunteer for anti-racism organisations

Many groups work tirelessly to combat racism and they often need volunteers. Lending your time and energy can make a significant impact.

8. Challenge racist policies

Identify and oppose policies at local, school, or national levels that disproportionately affect GEM people. Mobilise your peers, and seek to influence change through petitions, letters, and peaceful protests.

9. Celebrate diversity

Organise or participate in events that celebrate different cultures. Festivals, art shows, and food fairs can be fun and powerful ways to appreciate and learn about diverse traditions.

10. Be a mentor

Role modelling can have a profound influence, especially on younger peers. By mentoring, you can help nurture a generation that respects and appreciates racial diversity.

Challenging racism is no small task, but it's crucial for the wellbeing of individuals and our society. Remember, changing the world starts with our actions and choices. Each of the strategies outlined offers a pathway to a more just and inclusive community. Let's use these tools to build a world where diversity is celebrated and all people can thrive. Together, we can make a difference – step by step, action by action

Blackout Tuesday: the black square is a symbol of online activism for non-activists

An article from *The Conversation*.

By Jolynna Sinanan, Research Fellow in Digital Media and Ethnography, University of Sydney

Earlier this week, you might have seen your social media taken over by a stream of posts showing simple images of a black square. These posts, often tagged with #BlackoutTuesday, were gestures of solidarity with protests against the police killing of George Floyd in Minneapolis.

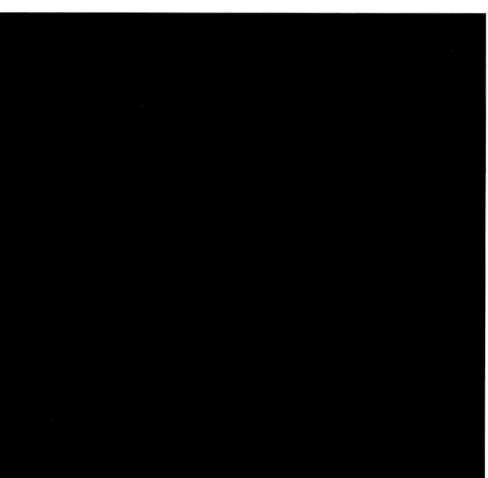

There have been more than 28 million of these posts on Instagram, and online services such as Spotify and Apple Music also joined the movement. Social media activism is nothing new, but the scale of #BlackoutTuesday showed not only the cause but also the method of the protest were distinctly 2020.

What was Blackout Tuesday?

Last weekend, two black women working in the music industry began a campaign asking the music industry, which they note 'has profited predominantly from Black art', to put its activities on hold for a day on Tuesday June 2.

Using the hashtag #theshowmustbepaused, they began making their case by posting an image to Instagram of a black background and white text asking the music industry to pause and reflect on the ways it disenfranchises black employees.

The movement soon took off: as the week began, posts showing simple black squares quickly proliferated across social media. The hashtags varied, from the original #theshowmustbepaused to #BlackLivesMatter and #blackouttuesday.

Strange effects of the black squares

The black square posts have come in many forms. Some show the square alone with no text, some with #BlackoutTuesday and others with #BlackLivesMatter, associating the trend with the established political movement.

Many captions and comments posted with the image express the poster's desire to educate themselves and others about racial inequality, to stand in solidarity with the wider Black Lives Matter movement, or simply 'to do better'.

While the trend gathered momentum with posts from US celebrities as well as ordinary people around the world, it also attracted criticism.

Criticisms include the use of the #BlackLivesMatter hashtag, which activists use to stay informed about demonstrations, for financial donations and to document racial violence by police. Filling the hashtag's feed with black squares, some argued, obscured more direct activities associated with the movement, redirected attention and 'silenced' activists.

The current situation

Despite the backlash, the sheer numbers of people around the world who have posted black squares indicates that #BlackoutTuesday is a form of political expression that has resonated with the particular moment of June 2020.

Several countries are just coming out of pandemic lockdowns that have lasted for weeks or months. These lockdowns have meant work, education, entertainment and political engagement have largely been experienced online.

The pandemic and the economic devastation in its wake have left millions of people feeling uncertain and helpless. And in this dismal environment, in the same week the US surpassed 100,000 Covid-19 deaths, George Floyd was killed by police like many other African-American men before him.

Why not everyone is an activist

From the Arab Spring uprisings of the early 2010s to the Hong Kong demonstrations of 2019–20, social media has become an essential tool for political action. Activists use it to organise demonstrations, generate debate and facilitate social change.

However, for many people outside Western, liberal democracies, and in the 'Global South', visible political engagement can have severe consequences. This is particularly true for those who are kept from freedoms and opportunities by systemic exclusion based on race, class, gender or sexuality.

These consequences range from professional or social exclusion to harassment and intimidation to outright persecution and detention. As a result, many people in such societies may subscribe to 'non-activism'.

Non-activism means explicitly rejecting visible involvement with political causes to focus on everyday concerns. People may reject activism even while they know doing so makes social change less likely.

Activism for non-activists

Blackout Tuesday was in some ways an ideal form of activism for non-activists, which may explain some of its enormous international popularity.

My own analysis of posts indicates users are based in countries including Ukraine, Brazil, and the Caribbean islands. Those who posted used visual social media to connect the experiences of one individual to structural violence and race-based exclusion that is pervasive in countries beyond the US.

The black square allowed millions of people to engage with a politically charged issue without having to seem too political themselves.

For many, especially those who would not consider themselves 'political', symbolism is a legitimate form of political engagement.

Worlds colliding

Algorithms, applications and automated systems play a significant role in what we see in online media. They affect how content reaches some audiences and not others, and automated systems may also perpetuate racial bias.

When activists turn to social media to further their cause, they too are ruled by the algorithms. We saw this in the criticisms of #BlackoutTuesday posts on Instagram, and particularly those using the #BlackLivesMatter hashtag, for preventing the hashtags (and the algorithms) from doing what protest organisers wanted them to do.

We may think of 'social media users' as collective audiences, but they are made up of individuals embedded in a variety of contexts who do not necessarily have much in common.

For seasoned activists, #BlackoutTuesday was a moment in which popular support paradoxically made it harder to keep people informed. But for many others, it may have been a step towards political engagement through difficult terrain.

4 June 2020

THE CONVERSATION

The above information is reprinted with kind permission from The Conversation.
© 2010-2024, The Conversation Trust (UK) Limited

www.theconversation.com

Performative allyship is deadly — here's what to do instead

Activism can't begin and end with a hashtag.

By Holiday Phillips

On May 25, George Floyd was murdered by a Minneapolis police officer who kneeled on his neck for more than eight minutes as Floyd gasped, 'I can't breathe.' On March 13, Breonna Taylor was shot dead by police who stormed her home as she slept. On February 25, Ahmaud Arbery was killed in the middle of the day by two white men, a retired policeman and his son. They got in their car, tailed him, and shot him twice.

I could go on.

These tragedies, just the most recent examples in a long history of violence against black people, have led to an explosion of attention on social media. In the days after Arbery's death, I scrolled through Instagram, reading post after post from white friends and influencers professing their outrage and disbelief. Urging us to #sayhisname. The posts were flooded with comments from more (mostly) white people, thanking them for their 'bravery' and praising them for 'speaking truth to power.' Three months after the shooting, Gregory McMichael and Travis McMichael were arrested and charged with murder in what has been heralded as a victory for the powers of social media, a place where normal citizens can 'use their voice' to demand justice.

Still, as a black woman, instead of feeling inspired by this act of solidarity, I found myself feeling angry and afraid. Looking through my feed, I wanted to say to my white friends, 'You're here now, but where are you the other 364 days a year when anti-racism isn't trending? When racism isn't tucked safely behind the screen in your hand, but right there in front of your face?'

I am not overlooking the fact that public allyship can help spur positive change. Voices can be heard, and some small version of justice may even be served as a result. But we must also not be lulled into believing that this kind of allyship is enough to dismantle the conditions that made it possible for an innocent black man to be lynched in broad daylight. And we must not let the kind of performative allyship that begins and ends with hashtags take centre stage in the quest for equality.

What is performative allyship?

To understand performative allyship, let's first look at what real allyship is. An ally is someone from a nonmarginalised group who uses their privilege to advocate for a marginalised group. They transfer the benefits of their privilege to those who lack it. Performative allyship, on the other hand, is when someone from that same nonmarginalised group professes support and solidarity with a marginalised group in a way that either isn't helpful or that actively harms that group. Performative allyship usually involves the 'ally' receiving some kind of reward – on social media, it's that virtual pat on the back for being a 'good person' or 'on the right side.'

I want to make clear that I do not exempt myself from this kind of behaviour. I myself have spoken online with fervent vigour about the evils of factory farming, only to later that day sneak a piece of cheese from my partner's plate. (If I didn't order it, I'm still vegan, right?) I understand the urge to say something, especially when people are reminding you that to be silent is to be complicit. But the problem with performative allyship is not that it in itself damages, but that it excuses. It excuses privileged people from making the personal sacrifices necessary to touch the depth of the systemic issues it claims to address. If you hashtagged #sayhisname, you've done your bit, right? You've publicly declared you stand against racism and therefore can check that off your to-do list. Wrong.

Looking through the Instagram stories of apparent white allies shouting for justice, my heart broke to see their posts immediately followed by photos of what they had for lunch or something similarly unrelated. This kind of allyship is transient. A passing story. A repost. For the 'gram. It's cheap and inauthentic.

How do you spot performative allyship?

On social media, there are four clues.

1. **The post is usually simple** – a few words, an image or whatever the going hashtag is (in the aesthetic of their personal brand, of course). Performative allyship refuses to engage with the complexity below the surface or say anything new.

2. **It almost always expresses itself as outrage, disbelief, or anger 'at the injustice.'** But your outrage isn't useful – if anything, it's a marker of your privilege, that to you racism is still surprising. Trust me when I say this is not so for black, indigenous, and people of colour (BIPOC) for whom racism is an everyday reality.

3. **It refuses to acknowledge any personal responsibility for the systemic issues that provided the context for the relevant tragedy.** Instead, it looks at a villain 'out there' – a crooked police officer or a heartless conservative. It separates you (good) from them (bad).

4. **Perhaps most noticeable, it's usually met with praise, approval, or admiration for the person expressing it.** That is its lifeblood.

If you recognise yourself in some of these descriptions, know that this doesn't mean I'm saying you don't care, or that you're a bad person, or a racist. Just that you've fallen into the trap of thinking that your activism can begin and end with a hashtag. But systemic racism doesn't care about your hashtags and your outrage. People have been hashtagging #BlackLivesMatter for eight years, and young black men are being killed in the street for jogging. It's critical to realise that if your allyship is performative, you are excusing yourself from engaging with the tough and messy conversations necessary to address the root causes. The conversations that will actually bring about change. And you're easing your guilt with the empty advocacy of keyboard warrioring when what you really need to be doing is advocating with your actions.

So what can you do instead? Here are some suggestions.

Act with your wallet

This, I believe, is the greatest thing you as a white person can do to support BIPOC. If you are disgusted by the centuries of state-sponsored theft from black, Asian, and indigenous people's lands, then support BIPOC-owned businesses. Initiate your own program of reparations by actively looking for products and services you use regularly and finding alternatives created by BIPOC. And if you're heartbroken by the exploitation of people of colour in some of the poorest countries in the world, refuse to buy from the fashion and technology companies that continue to shamelessly exploit adults and children in their labour practices.

Call out people in real life

It's easy to call people out when you're hidden behind a keyboard. You know what's hard? Calling out your boss when he routinely mixes up your two Indian colleagues, or facing off with your racist relative when they start talking about 'immigrants taking our jobs.' If you can't yet speak up, that's okay, but recognise that fact and commit to doing your work so that, one day soon, you can.

Inform yourself

It's all too easy to focus on the people 'out there' – the evil ones, the KKK, the neo-Nazis. Almost every sensible person believes these people and their views are deplorable. But because they are marginal and few in number, they have little power and influence over the mechanics of society. You know what does have mass influence? Systemic white apathy and privilege. And I'm sorry to say, if you're white, no matter how nice you are, unless you're doing serious and sustained personal anti-racism work, you are a part of the machine. Ask your BIPOC friends about their experiences of racism and listen. Engage in ways to confront your own biases. Read books on the history of racism in your country. (This reading list is a great place to start.)

Do something that no one will ever know

As Lil Wayne said, 'Real Gs move in silence like lasagne.' This is never more true than in activism. Sometimes real activism requires us to step up and shout. But far more often, it requires us to carry out simple daily acts that no one will ever see. If, on reflection, everything you do is public, it's likely you're a performative ally. Challenge yourself to do things quietly, like changing the things you buy, giving your platform to a BIPOC, or educating yourself on the history of racism without telling everyone about how educated you now are. That way, you know you're really down for the cause – and not the cause of looking like a woke person.

Simply 'saying stuff' is easy. You know what's hard? Not buying stuff you want because the supply chain is violent. Turning down a job because the company employs child labour in Africa. Calling out other white people when they say something clearly racist. That shit is hard. But if you want to be a true ally to BIPOC, you have to be willing to do it. Anyone can post hashtags on social media. And the fact that this is seen as an act of activism is deadly.

So this is a call. For all of us. To get honest and real. To look at how much we really care. To understand that when our allyship does more for ourselves than for the people it professes to help, we have a problem. Be an activist who actually acts. It's too late in the day to be anything but.

17 June 2020

The above information is reprinted with kind permission from Holiday Phillips.
© Holiday Phillips 2024

www.holidayphillips.com

Windrush scandal explained

Who are the Windrush generation?

The 'Windrush' generation are those who arrived in the UK from Caribbean countries between 1948 and 1973. Many took up jobs in the nascent NHS and other sectors affected by Britain's post-war labour shortage. The name 'Windrush' derives from the 'HMT Empire Windrush' ship which brought one of the first large groups of Caribbean people to the UK in 1948. As the Caribbean was, at the time, a part of the British commonwealth, those who arrived were automatically British subjects and free to permanently live and work in the UK.

What is the Windrush scandal?

The Windrush scandal began to surface in 2017 after it emerged that hundreds of Commonwealth citizens, many of whom were from the 'Windrush' generation, had been wrongly detained, deported and denied legal rights. *Guardian* journalist Amelia Gentleman investigated and began reporting their experiences. As these shocking stories hit the headlines, Caribbean leaders took the issue up with then-prime minister, Theresa May.

There was widespread shock and outrage at the fact that so many Black Britons had had their lives devastated by Britain's deeply flawed and discriminatory immigration system.

Why did the Windrush scandal happen?

Commonwealth citizens were affected by the Government's 'Hostile Environment' legislation – a policy announced in 2012 which tasked the NHS, landlords, banks, employers and many others with enforcing immigration controls. It aimed to make the UK unlivable for undocumented migrants and ultimately push them to leave.

Because many of the Windrush generation arrived as children on their parents' passports, and the Home Office destroyed thousands of landing cards and other records, many lacked the documentation to prove their right to remain in the UK. The Home Office also placed the burden of proof on individuals to prove their residency predated 1973. The Home Office demanded at least one official document from every year they had lived here. Attempting to find documents from decades ago created a huge, and in many cases, impossible burden on people who had done nothing wrong.

Falsely deemed as 'illegal immigrants'/'undocumented migrants' they began to lose their access to housing, healthcare, bank accounts and driving licenses. Many were placed in immigration detention, prevented from travelling abroad and threatened with forcible removal, while others were deported to countries they hadn't seen since they were children.

Their harmful and unjust treatment provoked widespread condemnation of Government's failings on the matter, with calls being made for radical reform of the Home Office and the UK's immigration policy. In response to these demands, then Home Secretary, Sajid Javid announced in May 2018 that the Home Office would commission a *Windrush Lessons Learned Review*.

The scandal is far from over

For those who have been affected by the Windrush scandal, justice has still not been done. There is a huge backlog of cases still to be resolved. The Windrush compensation scheme is a failure – it is complex to navigate, there is a lack of free legal advice, claims take months to process and compensation offers are insultingly small.

And the policies that led to this scandal are still in place. The 'Hostile Environment' – which bars those without the right papers from the safety net we all rely on – hasn't even been suspended for the duration of the Covid-19 outbreak, in spite of repeated calls for it, from those affected by the rules.

The Government promised to find the root causes of the Windrush scandal and learn lessons from it. Wendy Williams, His Majesty's Chief Inspector of the Constabulary, was tasked with carrying out an independent review. We, along with many others including lawyers, immigration advisors, local authorities, employers and charities, submitted evidence into what had happened, and why.

The review was finally published on 19 March 2020 – nearly two years since the scandal hit the headlines. The review makes absolutely clear that the Windrush scandal was not an accident, but the inevitable result of policies designed to make life impossible for those without the right papers.

This, coupled with decades of immigration legislation explicitly aimed at reducing non-white immigration from the Commonwealth, destroyed the lives of many black and minority ethnic British people.

Broken promises

In September 2020, the Home Office published an action plan, which the Home Secretary claimed would 'deliver for the Windrush generation' and usher in 'people-focused policies' at the department.

In practice, however, the plan lacks substance, is full of evasive language, and wilfully misinterprets recommendations from Wendy Williams' report. There is a failure to address the most important issues – like the hostile environment – head on, and there is a clear determination to maintain the status quo.

A report by the Home Affairs Select Committee, an influential group of MPs, in November 2021, found that only 5.8% of the people who are believed to be eligible for compensation have received a payment. And shockingly, 23 people have now died, never having seen a penny of the compensation they were owed.

And an independent report in March 2022 warns the department is running the risk of another Windrush-style scandal, if it fails to act now to make meaningful change to its culture, systems and policies.

In January 2023, Suella Braverman indicated that her department is abandoning the plan altogether. The Home Office is now backing out of key promises it made to 'right the wrongs' of the scandal.

June 2024

Activity

Research people who have been affected by the Windrush scandal and write a short biography of one of the people.

Research

Have there been any progress or updates on this scandal since this article was published? Look for recent news articles to see if the current Government has taken any recent action.

The above information is reprinted with kind permission from The Joint Council for the Welfare of Immigrants.
© 2024 JCWI

www.jcwi.org.uk

The Windrush generation hero who fought racism and won

In the 1960s train guard Asquith Xavier opposed a racist recruitment policy at Euston station, paving the way for workplace equality. But, says his granddaughter Camealia Xavier-Chihota, his legacy has been overlooked.

Nearly sixty years ago, in that momentous year when England last won the world cup, there was arguably an even more significant victory, one that would shape British employment law for years to come.

Not many people have heard the name Asquith Xavier.

Nearly six decades ago, the railway worker applied for a promotion that would see him move from Marylebone to Euston Station in 1966. But astonishingly, at the time there was an informal ban on Black workers holding railway jobs that would see them come into contact with the public, and he was turned down.

Determined

However, the determined Windrush generation member didn't take no for an answer.

He eventually overturned a racist recruitment policy at Euston station paving the way for equal opportunities in the workplace not only for other Windrush generation members but for Black Britons of the future.

Asquith Camile Xavier was born on July 18 1920, on the small Caribbean island of Dominica, then a British colony.

Like many members of the Windrush generation, he answered the British Government's call for those in the Caribbean to move to Britain to help rebuild its weakened economy following the end of the Second World War.

There were severe labour shortages, so Commonwealth citizens were invited to travel over to Britain. Asquith boarded the TN Ascania in his capital city of Roseau and docked in Southampton on April 16, 1958.

Settling in Paddington, West London, he shared lodgings with his sister Iola. The then 37-year-old had made prior arrangements to begin working at British Rail as a porter the very next day.

No stranger to hard work, Asquith spent the coming years tenaciously working his way up to become a guard at Marylebone railway station. Although he came to Britain alone, he soon sent for his wife Agnes and their children to join him in 1960.

He had become a well-respected man in his community and with his background in law enforcement, Asquith was often asked to assist fellow West Indians with official or legal matters, acting as a scribe and spokesperson on their behalf.

Discrimination

He would never disclose details of the overt discrimination faced by his fellow countrymen to his family, but bore it on his broad shoulders. Ever the optimist, Asquith saw the potential for race relations to improve in Britain for future generations.

He was a prim and particular man who knew the power of the first impression so his uniform was always spotless and his shoes shined to the highest standard.

In 1966, when the freight link at Marylebone depot was closed, he applied for a transfer to London Euston station. Asquith was told he was denied the job due to an unofficial colour bar which operated at the station, excluding Black people from working in customer-facing roles. Dissatisfied with this decision, he campaigned to end the racial discrimination practised by British Rail.

'His legacy has made a lasting impression on me and taught me that with matters of discrimination, the pen can be mightier than the sword'.

– Camealia Xavier-Chihota

The first Race Relations Act was passed a year before, in 1965, making it illegal to discriminate on the grounds of colour, race, ethnic or national origins in public places. But the railways, however, were not considered public.

His refusal to accept discrimination made history. Asquith's principled stance caught the attention of then home secretary Jim Callaghan.

Speaking about Asquith's case in parliament he said: 'The House has rarely faced an issue of greater social significance for our country and our children.'

Barbara Castle who was the transport secretary also took up the case. After she intervened British Rail abandoned its colour bar policies on July 15, 1966 and offered Asquith the job. The new post made him the first non-white train guard at Euston railway station.

Promotion

Not only did he secure the promotion, but his pay was backdated to when he had first applied for the position.

Subsequently, the Commission for Racial Equality was created.

His campaign also led to the strengthening of the Race Relations Act. In 1968, it became illegal to refuse housing, employment or public services to people because of their ethnic background.

On Asquith's first day working at Euston, his boss and station manager Ernest Drinnan was reported to have said: 'We expect Mr Xavier to fit in very well here… His record at Marylebone was exceptionally good and we know everyone here will take to him.'

Sadly, this wasn't quite the case. His victory came at a cost. He received race hate messages and threats to his life and required police protection on his way to and from work.

In 1972, Asquith and his family moved from London to Chatham in Kent, where he commuted daily by train to work at Euston station. But not long after, his health began to fail and in 1980, he passed away aged 59.

Describing my grandfather's journey to justice and his advancements in gaining equal opportunities for the non-white community in the workplace fills me with an overwhelming sense of pride.

Dignity

His dignity, strength of character and tenacity in the face of adversity makes me feel honoured to carry the Xavier name. His contribution to our society has undoubtedly shaped the way we live today and should be celebrated and never forgotten.

His legacy has made a lasting impression on me and taught me that with matters of discrimination, the pen can be mightier than the sword.

Asquith's stand against injustice helped reshape employment laws, empowering the Windrush generation who faced overt racism and paved the way to equality in the workplace for future generations.

The pandemic of 2020, and the shocking death of George Floyd, captured on video, highlighted ongoing racism globally. The backlash from the Black Lives Matter movement spotlighted Britain's racial injustices, marking a pivotal moment in time.

That summer I co-founded a charity with the goal of delivering supplementary education to fill the gaps in the national curriculum, empowering children with a broader view of history and modern society.

Medway Culture Club is run by a diverse team of volunteers including educators, industry professionals and community activists, we deliver workshops and events to the local community and schools to promote diversity and equality through inclusion, and counteract bias.

It's often the case that bias is sustained by a lack of racial literacy training and diversity in the curriculum.

While acknowledging the contribution of the Windrush generation is important, if achievements such as Asquith's are not more widely taught of or publicised, this undermines these acknowledgements, making them feel more like tokenistic Black History Month box ticks.

Pioneers

I feel my grandfather's impactful legacy has been lost in time. To progress, society must recognise the work of those who have bravely challenged the status quo. Limiting teaching Black history to one month isn't enough; it should be integrated across various subjects throughout the year.

To cultivate a more unified and accepting society, the national curriculum should include the achievements and contributions made by ethnically diverse people, like my grandfather and their impact on the nation.

Schools should include a broader, more accurate representation of history including the history of Windrush and the pioneers of that generation who came to rebuild a post-war Britain and launch the National Health Service.

What my grandfather was able to achieve and show people nearly 60 years ago, was not just that Black Lives Matter but that the quality of life of Black people matters equally.

6 May 2024

The above information is reprinted with kind permission from *The Voice*.
© 2024 GV Media Group Ltd.

www.voice-online.co.uk

How to be anti-racist

In recent years, you've probably heard a lot about racism and the importance of standing up against it. You might even have heard people say, 'I'm not racist.' But there's a big difference between being not racist and being anti-racist. Understanding this difference is a crucial first step in helping to make the world a fairer place.

Not racist vs. Anti-racist

Being 'not racist' is a passive position. It means that you don't actively participate in racist behaviour or say openly racist things. It might sound like a good stance, but it's not enough. Imagine standing by while someone bullies another person without stepping in – just because you're not the one bullying doesn't make the situation okay. It's the same with racism. Racism doesn't only come in the form of slurs or violence; it can be subtle, like unfair stereotypes or unequal opportunities based on someone's skin colour.

On the other hand, being anti-racist is an active choice. It means recognising that racism exists in many parts of society and doing something about it. Anti-racism involves challenging racist ideas, systems, and behaviours, even if they don't directly affect you. It's about speaking up when you see injustice, learning about different cultures and histories, and reflecting on how we might unknowingly support racism through our actions or beliefs.

How to be anti-racist

Educate yourself

A great way to start your journey as an anti-racist is by educating yourself about racism. This could mean reading books, watching documentaries, or listening to podcasts that focus on race and inequality. It's important to understand that racism isn't just about individuals being mean to one another. It's often built into systems like education, housing, and law enforcement, in ways that can be harder to spot. For example, statistics show that people from minority ethnic backgrounds in the UK are more likely to face discrimination in job hiring or be treated unfairly by the police.

Books like *Why I'm No Longer Talking to White People About Race* by Reni Eddo-Lodge can be a good starting point for understanding these issues in the UK context.

Challenge stereotypes

Stereotypes are harmful because they reduce people to one idea or label. You might hear someone say, 'All people from this background act like that,' or 'People from that country are always like this.' These kinds of statements are usually based on false assumptions. Challenge stereotypes when you hear them. You could say something like, 'I don't think that's true for everyone,' or ask the person to think about whether their idea is based on facts.

Call out racism

It's not always easy, but when you see someone making a racist comment or treating others unfairly, it's important to speak up. This doesn't have to mean starting an argument. You could say something like, 'That joke isn't funny, it's hurtful,' or 'I don't think what you said was fair.' If you're worried about confrontation, try talking to a teacher or another trusted adult who can help. Staying silent only allows racism to continue.

Support people of colour

Being anti-racist also means showing support for people who are impacted by racism. This could mean amplifying the voices of people of colour, whether by sharing their stories on social media or participating in events that focus on equality and justice. It's important to remember that racism isn't just an issue in the past. It's something that continues to affect people today, and everyone has a role in making things better.

Reflect on your own biases

Finally, being anti-racist means examining our own thoughts and behaviours. It can be uncomfortable to realise we might have biases, but everyone does. The key is to recognise them and work to overcome them. Ask yourself: Do I treat people differently based on their race? Do I have assumptions about certain groups? The more we question our own thinking, the better we can grow.

Conclusion

Being anti-racist is about more than just not being racist. It's about actively working to make society fairer for everyone. By educating yourself, challenging stereotypes, speaking up, and supporting people of colour, you can be part of the solution. Small actions can lead to big changes, and everyone can contribute to creating a more just and equal world.

Ways to fight against racism

Respect difference

And combat the 'I don't see race/colour' argument. We are all shaped by different life experiences, circumstances and our identity. Our gender, race, sexuality, religion, class, nationality all combines to make us who we are. It's important to celebrate people as they are and not try to diminish or invalidate their experience.

Read

Read books written by authors who have experienced racism or explore a viewpoint you may not have experienced directly. Reading not only builds knowledge and confidence in language to use around race, but also allows us to build empathy for others.

Listen

Be open to hearing about other people's experiences.

Talk about racism

Talking about racism plays a huge role in fighting against it. Having discussions in school or college, as well as with family and friends around race helps develop our understanding

Understand your privilege

White privilege is systemic in our society. It is a term coined to describe advantage given to white people over non-white people based on race.

Consider about what privileges you have based on your race and how these play a part in your day-to-day life. When has your appearance made you feel unsafe? Are there spaces you do not feel welcome? Have you found it easy to buy products for your skin tone, i.e., plasters. Do you often see yourself represented in TV shows or movies?

You could also think about what privileges you have based on your gender, sexuality, class, ability, religion, etc.

Speak out

If you see, hear, or read something that is racist, speak out against it (without putting yourself at risk). Even if it's only a 'joke', saying you don't agree when you hear something racist, will help others to see that it is not okay. Whether it is in person or online, challenge racism when you see it.

Don't take the abuse

If you feel someone is being racist towards you, seek help from a trusted adult, parent, friend, family member, or teacher.

Document and report online abuse

Most social media platforms have a 'Report Abuse' button if you are experiencing online abuse.

You can also block individual users, as well as close the app or walking away from your device. Tell a trusted friend, adult, family member or teacher if you are concerned about online bullying or harassment.

Know your rights

Everyone has the right to live freely without discrimination based on your race, ethnicity, and nationality. This is one of nine protected characteristics covered under the Equality Act 2010 discrimination law.

Further Reading/Useful Websites

Useful websites

www.cam.ac.uk

www.davidrobertsonline.org

www.holidayphillips.com

www.hud.ac.uk

www.independent.co.uk

www.jcwi.org.uk

www.manchester.ac.uk

www.morningstaronline.co.uk

www.telegraph.co.uk

www.theconversation.com

www.theguardian.com

www.voice-online.co.uk

www.yougov.co.uk

Further Reading

Books*

Why I'm no longer talking to White people about race – Reni Eddo-Lodge

How to be an Antiracist – Ibram X. Kendi

The Uncomfortable Truth about Racism – John Barnes

Windrush Child – Benjamin Zephaniah

This Book Is Anti-Racist – Aurélia Durand & Tiffany Jewel

100 Great Black Britons – Patrick Vernon

The Good Immigrant – Nikesh Shukla

Homecoming: Voices of the Windrush Generation – Colin Grant

Let Me Tell You This – Nadine Aisha Jassat

* Please note that these books are intended for a wide range of age-groups. Please ask your librarian for age-appropriate books.

Documentaries

Black and British: A Forgotten History – Available on BBC iPlayer

Maya Angelou: And Still I Rise (2017)

Glossary

Antisemitism
Antisemitism is hostility to, prejudice towards, or discrimination against Jews.

BAME
An acronym which stands for Black, Asian and Minority Ethnic backgrounds.

Demographics
Statistical characteristics of a population: for example, age, race or employment status.

Discrimination
Unfair treatment of someone because of the group/class they belong to.

Ethnic minority
A group of people who are different in their ancestry, culture and traditions from the majority of the population.

Ethnicity
Ethnicity is a concept used to categorise groups of people based on common cultural traits, such as language, religion, national origin, and ancestral customs. Unlike race, which is often perceived and defined based on physical characteristics, ethnicity is more closely tied to cultural identity and heritage

Global Ethnic Majority (GEM)
Global Ethnic Majority (GEM) is a collective term for people of Indigenous, African, Asian, or Latin American descent, who constitute approximately 85% of the global population.

Gypsies and travellers
Gypsies and travellers have traditionally pursued a nomadic lifestyle which involves moving around from place to place. English gypsies and Irish travellers are protected under the Race Relations Act. This is because they are members of a community with a shared history stretching back over hundreds of years and are recognised by the law as a distinct ethnic minority group.

Harassment
Usually persistent (but not always), a behaviour that is intended to cause distress and offence. It can occur on the school playground, in the workplace and even at home.

Hate Crime
Hate Crime is criminal behaviour where the perpetrator is motivated by hostility or demonstrates hostility towards the victim's disability, race, religion, sexual orientation or transgender identity. These things are 'protected characteristics'. A hate crime can include verbal abuse, intimidation, threats, harassment, assault and bullying, as well as damage to property.

Human rights
The basic rights all human beings are entitled to, regardless of who they are, where they live or what they do. Concepts of human rights have been present throughout history, but our modern understanding of the term emerged as a response to the horrific events of the Holocaust. While some human rights, such as the right not to be tortured, are absolute, others can be limited in certain circumstances: for example, someone can have their right to free expression limited if it is found they are guilty of inciting racial hatred.

Multiculturalism
A number of different cultures coexisting side-by-side, for example within a school or a country.

Race
The concept of race has evolved over time and varies across different cultural and geographic contexts. The categorisation is often based on characteristics such as skin colour, facial features, hair texture, and ancestry. While these characteristics are biological, the importance placed upon them and the meanings attached to them are created by societies and cultures.

Racial discrimination
Racial discrimination occurs when a person is treated less favourably because of their colour, race, nationality or ethnic or national origins.

Racial prejudice
The belief and prejudgment that one race is inferior to another. Feeling hatred towards another race just because they are different.

Racism
The belief that one race is superior to another / behaving in a negative or harmful way to someone because of their race.

Reverse discrimination
When trying to address social inequalities, sometimes reverse discrimination occurs. This occurs when discrimination is directed towards the dominant group in society, in order to favour the usually disadvantaged minority group.

Systemic racism
Also known as 'institutional racism'. This term refers to racism that is built into the structure of society and different institutions (e.g. schools, police, government).

The Race Relations Act 1976
The Race Relations Act 1976 is concerned with people's actions and the effects of their actions, not their opinions or beliefs. The Act makes it unlawful to racially discriminate against anyone. Racial discrimination is when someone treats a person less favourably because of their colour, race, nationality or ethnic or national origins. Racial discrimination is not the same as racial prejudice. It is not necessary to prove that the other person intended to discriminate against you: you only have to show that you received less favourable treatment as a result of what they did. The Race Relations Act 1976 also aims to promote race equality and good race relations.

Xenophobia
A fear of or hostility to foreigners, people from different cultures or strangers.

Index

A
actions to combat racism
    campaigning 38–39
    personal 31, 34–35, 40, 41
    and protest 9
    social media 32–33
African descent, people of 29–30
allyship 34–35
assaults, racist 15, 27

B
BAME 11, 18
Black British people 17–19
#BlackLivesMatter 8, 32, 35
#Blackout Tuesday 32–33
British identity 9, 17, 24–25

C
Child Q 12–13
Covid-19 12, 27

E
education to combat racism 39
educational attainment 18
Empire 24–25, 26
England flag 17, 20–21, 22
environmental racism 4
ethnicity 3, 6
Europe, prevalence of racism in 29–30
Evidence for Equality National Survey 14–15, 27

F
flags, national 17, 20–21, 22
Floyd, George 6, 34

G
global majority 11

H
health and healthcare 12, 17, 18–19
history of racial thinking 2, 6–8, 9

I
indigenous culture 24
institutional racism 4, 5, 25
integration 8–9

J
Jewish people 14–15

L
language, use of 11, 18, 25–26
laws on race discrimination 10, 38–39

M
media representation 18

P
perpetrators and victims 12–13 *see also* white people
police, British 5, 9, 10, 12–13, 19, 30
police, United States 23
political representation 19

R
resisting racism 8–9
riots 9

S
sexuality 18
social media 32–33, 34
St. George's Cross 17, 20–21, 22
structural racism 4, 5, 8, 26

T
tolerance 25–26
Traveller, Gypsy and Roma communities 14–15, 16, 28
types of racism 2, 4

U
United States 9, 23

V
victims and perpetrators 12–13 *see also* white people

W
White Fragility 26
white people
    as perpetrators 6–8, 12–13, 24
    as victims 14–15. *see also* Traveller, Gypsy and Roma communities
Windrush 36–37, 38
work and businesses 19, 30, 38

X
Xavier, Asquith Camile 38–39